THE GIRLS' BICYCLE HANDBOOK

EVERYTHING YOU NEED TO KNOW ABOUT LIFE ON TWO WHEELS

CAZ NICKLIN

Contents

PREFACE:
Women and the Bicycle   6

How to . . .

1. Get started   17
2. Find a bike you like   22
3. Accessorize your ride   48
4. Maintain your bike   74
5. Keep your bike secure   104
6. Cycle safely   118
7. Cycle in style   138
8. Cycle to work   168
9. Cycle for fun   184
10. Cycle to keep fit   204

Little Black Book of
Bicycle Style   220

Index   222

Women and the Bicycle

'Let me tell you what I think of bicycling. I think it has done more to emancipate women than anything else in the world. It gives women a feeling of freedom and self-reliance. I stand and rejoice every time I see a woman ride by on a wheel . . . the picture of free, untrammelled womanhood.'
Susan B. Anthony, American women's rights activist, 1896

The humble bicycle had a profound impact on the liberation of women. Initially, there was great objection to women riding bicycles – it was not deemed ladylike, and the brave few who cycled in the street were seen as outcasts or circus freaks. But, despite the disdain and disapproval, women persisted to cycle. The critics were fighting a losing battle.

By the 1890s, women were taking to their bicycles in droves in the US, France and in the UK, and it was this fast-spreading eagerness to ride 'the wheel' that caused fundamental and long-awaited changes to what women wore. Pre-bicycle women were expected to dress a certain way: their everyday wear consisting of a tight and restrictive corset and huge, floor-length skirt, not to mention layers and layers of underwear and petticoats that could amount to as much as a stone in weight. Can you imagine cycling your commute in such attire?

No, thank you. Well, this is exactly what our Victorian ancestors thought and, after a surge of bicycling accidents due to the ridiculously unsuitable clothes, the dress reform movement came to a head.

The most significant change was women shedding their skirts and instead sporting bloomers to cycle in. Bloomers were voluminous shorts made from wool or tweed that puffed out to give a feminine feel but tapered just above the ankle to allow movement. They got their name from American feminist Amelia Bloomer, who had championed the idea of a divided skirt in the women's liberation paper *The Lily* in the early 1850s. The idea had been deemed absurd by most at the time, and it was not until some 30 years later, when the bicycle became more commonplace, that the bloomer finally had its day. The British Rational Dress Society fought tirelessly on the matter and in 1889 one member, Charlotte Carmichael Stope, made an impromptu speech on the subject of rational dress at a meeting of the British Association for the Advancement of Science, and it became a huge news story. The seed had been sown in women's minds, the skirts came off and the bloomers went on – the first real step towards women wearing trousers.

Riding a bike gave women a chance to exercise and get out in the fresh air – such simple pleasures that they were often denied. Women were seen as fragile, weak creatures and it was thought that physical exertion was bad for their health, despite the fact that many working-class women worked long hours in very physical jobs. Initially, women were believed to be far too delicate to handle these new 'machines' and it was claimed that the cycling position would either arouse them (not allowed in Victorian times) or prevent them from having children. But women got a taste for the physical exhilaration – the sheer thrill of riding a bike outdoors – as well as realizing that exercise made them feel good, and eventually they stuck two Victorian fingers up at the stuffy conformists.

Cycling also allowed women to go places on their own, another fundamental freedom that, from a modern standpoint, it seems extraordinary to have had to live without. Young women of the middle and upper classes were not allowed to go anywhere by themselves and were always chaperoned, especially when meeting members of the opposite sex. But the bike enabled them to travel alone or at least cycle away from their chaperones! This was not a freedom exclusive to those with stature and money – it also gave working-class women freedom and mobility, enabling them to get to school or work and to get out and socialize.

The bicycle gave women a taste of independence and freedom, and it made their minds, bodies and wills stronger. It was heralded as a freedom machine and seen by many suffragettes as a powerful force in the fight to get the vote. As Elizabeth Cady Stanton said, 'Woman is riding to suffrage on a bicycle.'

HEROINES OF CYCLING

Blanche d'Antigny (1840–74)

Blanche d'Antigny, a star of French theatre and opera, was one of the first women to be captured on canvas with a bicycle. Blanche did not hold back when it came to her personal life either, running away from home aged 14 with a lover and having a series of high-profile affairs throughout her short life. Women riding velocipedes in public were frowned upon in the early days and it was only the very plucky who dared to have a go – 'French actresses' being cited as the type of women that would.

Lady Harberton (1843–1911)

Lady Harberton, Florence Wallace Pomeroy, was the wife of a British Viscount and President of the Western Rational Dress Society… and an avid cyclist. In 1898, when out for a bike ride, dressed boldly in bloomers and a short riding jacket, she stopped off for some lunch at the Hautboy Hotel, Ockham, Surrey. She was, however, refused entrance to the restaurant for indecent dress. The CTC (Cyclists' Touring Club), still going today, attempted to sue the establishment for refusing food to a traveller but unfortunately lost the case. Hopefully, this did not stop Lady Harberton wearing her modern cycling get-up. Somehow, I doubt it did.

Sarah Grand (1854–1943)

The British Sarah Grand was born Frances Clarke but assumed her new name when she reinvented herself as a feminist writer. Her novels and treatises were considered key to establishing and promoting the ideal of the 'New Woman' – a modern woman who was educated, had a career and refused to follow the dictates of a male-dominated society. Grand was a keen cyclist, her central characters cycled and she often gave talks to women about the benefits of cycling. She was interviewed in cycling magazines of the time and was a strong supporter of rational dress: 'The New Woman has too much healthy enjoyment of life to worry about whether her ankles are visible or not. Besides, she has such good ones – and naturally she knows it.'

Annie Londonderry (1870–1947)

Annie Londonderry, a Jewish-American mother of three, left her husband and children to cycle around the world for a bet – a rather hefty bet of $5,000 – at the age of 25. It was thought a woman could not achieve such a feat, but she made the trip successfully in just 15 months. She set off with only her bike, a single change of clothes and a pistol, and she earned her money as she went by wearing advertising boards as she cycled. She even changed her surname to Londonderry (from Cohen Kopchovsky), to promote the name of the water company that was sponsoring the ride. She was also reported to be quite a show-woman, entertaining crowds at her various stop-offs around the globe. On her return, she became a journalist for the *New York World*, claiming she could do anything a man could do.

Alfonsina Strada (1891–1959)

Alfonsina Strada was born into a peasant family in Castelfranco Emilia in Italy. She is said to have been a tomboy as a child and showed talent and enthusiasm for riding a bike from an early age, winning her first race at the age of 13 (her prize was a live pig). In 1915 she married but, instead of settling down, the couple moved to Milan where Alfonsina rode in the velodrome and her husband became her trainer. In 1924 she controversially raced in Giro D'Italia, where she went under the name of Alfonsin and was believed to be a man. The truth came out the day before the race and despite much objection she was allowed to take part. She started off well but on the second day was subject to horrendous weather and she crashed, breaking her handlebars. Alfonsina was reported to have been given a broomstick by a peasant to use as a replacement handlebar and carried on racing but unfortunately finished outside of the time limit, as did many of the male cyclists. Alfonsina set a women's world record for covering 32 kilometres in an hour, which remained unbeaten for many years. In later life, she swapped the bicycle for a motorbike and tragically died when, returning home from watching a bike race, the motorbike fell on her and she suffered a heart attack.

Beryl Burton (1937–96)

Beryl Burton has been heralded as one of the most successful cyclists of all time yet she never became a household name. She was at the top of her game for 25 years, winning 90 domestic championships, 7 world

championships and setting a record for the 12-hour time trial that beat the men's record for two years. However, despite this great success, her life was far from glamorous and she worked full time at a rhubarb farm throughout her cycling career. Born and bred in Yorkshire, Beryl married Charlie Burton aged 17. Charlie was a cyclist himself and he encouraged Beryl to get into the sport; realizing her talent, he became her coach and they were a winning team for many years. They had a daughter, Denise, who became a cyclist herself, and mother and daughter raced against each other on a national level and raced in the same Team GB in the World Championships in 1972. Four days before her 59th birthday, Beryl died of heart failure while out on a training ride.

Victoria Pendleton (b. 1980)

Pendleton was born into a cycling family and has been on a bike since she was a tot. Her dynamic performance and open and honest personality has made her hugely popular and

the age of 21. Laura and her teammates Dani King and Joanna Roswell not only took the gold at the Olympics but beat the world record for the team track pursuits six consecutive times that year. Laura also won gold for the omnium, an individual track event where contestants compete in six different disciplines, and in 2013 was awarded an OBE. She continues to be a world-class cyclist at the top of her game.

she is one of a group of athletes who have brought cycling back into fashion as a sport. Despite showing great promise in her early career, she was known to struggle with her self-esteem and has admitted to finding the pressures of the sport extremely hard and was on the verge of giving up. Luckily, she turned a corner when she started working with a psychiatrist who helped her fight off the negativity and go for gold. With her all-new positive outlook, she went from strength to strength and has won nine world titles and a record six for individual sprint, retiring on a high with a gold medal for the keirin racing at the 2012 Olympics.

Laura Trott (b. 1992)

Laura Trott was born a month prematurely with a collapsed lung and suffered from asthma as a child. She only started cycling aged seven when her mum took up the sport to lose weight: a humble beginning for a young woman who would go on to be a double Olympic gold medallist before

How to . . .
Get started

Cycling can have such a positive impact on your everyday life. My journey to work was transformed from a stressful rush on public transport to an invigorating bicycle ride, and I was hooked. It won't all be plain sailing, but with a positive attitude and a willingness to learn you will overcome these barriers and reap the fantastic benefits.

The decision to start was primarily practical – I was fed up with feeling claustrophobic on the tube or risking unpredictable bus journeys that left me rushing into work a flustered and apologetic mess. I had been contemplating cycling for a while, so one sunny weekend in March I bit the bullet and bought a bike. Within a month, I had become utterly bewitched by the bicycle. Not only was I arriving at work promptly, but I was physically and mentally energized – I felt like shouting from the rooftops just how wonderful my new mode of transport was. The humble bicycle, which had been my partner-in-crime as a child, was an equally good friend to me now.

BENEFITS

So just what is it about riding a bike? Here's ten reasons why cycling makes so much sense for the modern girl about town.

Save money

Cycling is free! Yes, you need to buy a bike and a few accessories but this can be done on a budget. Set off on your bike with a packed lunch and you can actually go a whole day without spending a single penny – a liberating feeling in an age where we seem to have to open our wallets the minute we leave the house. Think about how much you spend on public transport or petrol in a week – and then a year. Cycling even half of those journeys could save you hundreds, if not thousands of pounds.

Get fit: healthy body and heart

If, like me, you don't get along with the gym and don't have time to commit to a regular sport (or just aren't interested in one!), cycling can be the perfect way to fit some exercise into your daily routine. Because the

bicycle supports your weight, it gets your body moving without too much strain. It's also a great way to burn calories, as you can cycle for a relatively long period of time without getting completely puffed out – and it's the perfect type of aerobic exercise for your heart. Once you get started, you may find you want to push yourself and get involved in longer rides or even races, or you may be happy just pootling – it's entirely up to you!

Improve your well-being

Your mental health is just as important as your physical health, and exercise is key to keeping both in good shape. Many women I've talked to say cycling makes them feel happier, often transforming their mood at the start or end of the day. I entirely agree. I can often make a correlation between feeling

blue and a lack of bicycle time. Exercising releases endorphins and this, combined with fresh air and the sheer fun of riding a bike, can truly lift your mood.

Avoid public transport

As a city girl, I do have huge respect for public transport, but it's a love/hate relationship that sometimes leaves me tearing my hair out! Whether it's being scrunched up against someone's sweaty back in a hot, cramped train, or waiting for what seems like hours in the rain for a bus – there's no doubt that public transport can be a painful chore. So, if you want to escape the rush-hour crowds or the futile waiting and just get yourself home, take your journey into your own hands and cycle.

Look after the environment

We all talk about being greener but, apart from doing a spot of recycling, how many of us actually take action? There may not be a great deal the average person can do about deforestation but one thing we can do is drive less. Cars are accountable for ten per cent of our carbon footprint. They also cause air and noise pollution, not to mention congestion and aggression in our towns and cities. Cycling regularly instead of using the car is a proactive step to living a greener life – rather than just talking about it!

Meet people

Cycling can be a great way to meet people and make friends. When I first started cycling, I felt I'd become part of a community who looked out for each other – a friendly gang. Whether it's chatting to other cyclists on the commute, taking part in an event or joining a group, there's no denying that cycling is sociable – and you can get as involved as you want. I am not saying all cyclists are friendly but there is a reassuring camaraderie among most, and over the years I have made some good friends and met many like-minded people through cycling.

Enjoy the fresh air and sense of freedom

I used to work long hours in an office and often felt drained and depleted after spending so much time indoors. Cycling was the perfect remedy. I felt invigorated, having had a healthy dose of fresh air each day, and there was a wonderful sense of freedom in striking out on my own, just me and my bike against the world. I also felt more in touch with the weather and the seasons – and I don't just mean I got wet when it rained! That first hint of spring in the air or the crackle of autumn leaves under your wheels can be a life-affirming delight.

Save time and be on time

One of the beauties of cycling is that it's faster than walking, usually quicker than driving for local trips, and not subject to the unpredictability and delays of public transport. You can normally guarantee how long a journey is going to take you, so you can avoid stumbling into work late. The bike is also a highly efficient way of running all your errands. I was once without my bike for a while, and I couldn't believe how much longer all my regular trips and local errands took without it. The bike is a bad-ass time-saver.

Discover your town or city

For me, this was one of the most unexpected rewards of cycling. I got an enormous amount of satisfaction in discovering and understanding the geography of my own city: a sense of pride in knowing my way around and a delight in finding small, pretty streets that I would never have come across otherwise. This sense of independent discovery is one of the greatest joys of cycling.

Look fabulous

There is just something inherently stylish about a woman on a bicycle. Although my initial reasons for cycling were practical, it was seeing a wonderfully elegant lady in a dress, gliding through the park on a Dutch-style bicycle that finally convinced me. I went out and bought a bike that weekend. And I am definitely not alone in my thinking. 'Cycle chic' blogs, capturing women looking stylish on bikes, are an international phenomenon, and women on bikes are used to sell many fashion brands, from Topshop to Chanel. This doesn't mean riding your bike needs to be a fashion show, but just that you can look great on a bike – you don't need to wrap yourself in layers of Lycra and shiny Day-Glo.

BARRIERS

As much as there are real *benefits* to cycling there are also real *barriers*. I've given you many points in favour of cycling but I won't deny that there are also plenty of reasons to be put off.

My barriers felt mountainous: as a non-driver the prospect of cycling through the city's busy streets filled me with fear. I was also a fashion-conscious 26-year-old and had no desire to wear ugly, unflattering cycling gear.

Having spoken to many women who don't cycle, the most common phrase I hear is, 'I *would* like to cycle but . . .' They like the idea but they have a handful of reasons why they feel they can't. Take a look at the common barriers below. Do any look familiar? If so, don't panic – with a little bit of work, you can nip these worries in the bud and be cycling with a smile on your face in no time.

I would like to cycle but . . .

I am terrified of cycling in traffic

This is the most common fear that puts women (and men) off cycling. The first thing to note here is that cycling is often a particularly bad advert for itself – we see city cyclists weaving in and out of busy traffic, taking risks, running red lights and so on. But you don't have to be this type of cyclist. Before you take to the streets, I would highly recommend professional cycle training – just as drivers need training, so do cyclists. Then, start slowly on quieter roads to get your confidence up. Once you understand the rules of the road and have some experience under your belt, your confidence and skill will grow, and it won't be long before you will be looking back with pride at how far you've come. See *Cycle safely*, p118.

I don't want to get hot and sweaty and have to change at work

One cunning way to avoid the hassle of getting changed at work is by not having to get changed at work! Invest in a utility bike that's not designed for speed, and then cycle at a leisurely pace – and you can remain in the same outfit all day, odour and sweat free. The invasion of sporty cycling into popular culture has led us to believe that we must cycle fast, inevitably working up a sweat, but that's not a practical way to get to work. In countries such as Holland and Denmark, bikes are the main mode of transport for millions and they wouldn't dream of setting off in different clothes. Be part of cycling's new cultural shift – slow down; it's not a race. See *Find a bike you like*, p22.

I have too much stuff to carry

Whether it's a handbag, shopping, a laptop or party shoes, us girls very rarely leave the house without stuff to carry. There's a huge myth that it's difficult to carry things on a bike. In fact, quite the opposite is true. With a combination of panniers and a basket, you can carry quite substantial amounts of stuff on your bike, and it's much easier than hauling it all about on foot, as the bike takes the weight, not you. See *Accessorize your ride*, p48.

I don't want to look like a 'cyclist'

In recent years this has been a major barrier, putting many women off cycling. At some point in the 1990s, a ridiculous uniform appeared, consisting of Lycra cycling shorts or leggings, bright yellow hi-viz anoraks and weird angular helmets that stripped even the coolest of their style status. Most new cyclists felt that they had to conform and throw their femininity out the window. As a result, understandably, hordes of women turned their noses up at cycling. But it doesn't have to be like this! You can cycle in your own tasteful clothes and find accessories to match. Cycling can be a way to express your personal style, rather than hamper it. See *Cycle in style*, p138.

My bike is broken and I don't know how to fix it

What is it about broken things? We know they need fixing but we develop a mental block about doing anything about it. And the longer you leave it, the harder it gets, so what's needed here is a polite kick up the bottom. Here are some proactive options. All you need to do is choose one, stick to it and you've hurdled the problem.

1. If your bike is old and decrepit and you don't feel excited by the thought of riding it, sell it or recycle it and then treat yourself to a new set of wheels.

2. If your bike has been slumped in the corner of the garage and makes noises when you try to ride it, either:
a) book it straight in for a service and get the problems sorted by a professional; or
b) do the M check in *Maintain your bike*. Put a weekend aside and see if you can fix it yourself. It may just need minor tweaks, like oiling or a puncture repair, which can be easily carried out at home, saving you money. See *Maintain your bike*, p74.

I'm worried I'll get lost

Finding your way can feel a little scary when you're starting out, but you'll soon find your regular routes – and gain satisfaction from doing so. The key is to start with local trips and build up from that – the thrill of discovery will quickly replace any fears about getting lost. We are also lucky to live in an age where technology is a huge help. Whether it's checking routes online or following GPS maps on your phone, finding your way is easier than ever before. See *Cycle to work*, p168.

I don't have anywhere to keep my bike at home

Having no obvious place to put your bike at home can create a logistical puzzle, but don't let this beat you. Explore all the possible options for what type of bike you ride and where to keep it – whether it's opting for a folding bike, sneaking your road bike behind the sofa or securely fastening your utility bike to the wall outside, you WILL find a way to park your ride. See *Find a bike you like*, p22, and *Keep your bike secure*, p104.

'I finally concluded that all failure was from a wobbling will rather than a wobbling wheel.'
Frances E. Willard, *Wheel Within a Wheel: How I learned to Ride the Bicycle*, 1895

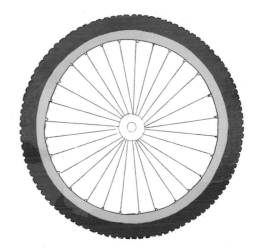

PROFILE

Jenny Livingstone, Tasmania

Blog: iwanttoridemy.blogspot.com

What bike do you ride and why do you like it?

I ride a Schwinn Jenny 7-speed, which gently got the adult, non-driving me back into bicycles after more than a decade. Not to mention it was blue and it literally had my name on it! Having not seen a bicycle since the 1990s, the revo shifter amazed me. Now I also own a Pashley Princess Sovereign in Buckingham Black, a 1980s Repco Traveller and a new Scott Contessa Speedster road bike.

Where do you cycle and what's the cycle scene like?

My spouse and I live in Burnie — a tiny, semi-rural beach city in Tasmania that has only one shared path and it doesn't yet connect to our neighbours, so I'm bound by an intimidating national highway, unless we drive the bicycles to the next town.

The Tasmanian cycling community is currently pretty sport-dominated but the state has a rich cycling history; you can tour most of it by bicycle, either guided or alone (a future goal of mine), and it even holds the largest Penny Farthing races in the world. Lately, I'm seeing more family groups, older couples and young women on bikes. Beach cruisers are having a moment. The inventor of Bike Hour (a pro-bicycling protest) lives in Tasmania, so there's hope for us yet.

How does cycling benefit you?

I'm a life-long pedestrian/public transport user so the main benefit for me is being timetable free and carrying heavy loads on my bicycle that would otherwise be a struggle on foot. Also it's NEVER NOT FUN.

What's your favourite outfit to cycle in?

My wardrobe has changed drastically since I reintroduced myself to bicycles. I used to be mostly jeans based but now I wear a lot more dresses because they give me maximum freedom of movement around the hips and legs (while also preventing bum-crack exposure). I look at dresses and skirts differently when I'm shopping, dividing them into 'good bike' and 'bad bike' depending upon how stretchy or wide they are from the thighs to the knees.

Any other thoughts on cycling?

I'd love to see even more women, children and transportation cyclists in Australia. Every year, new paths and facilities pop up, so don't be afraid to get back into bicycling. The magical thing about riding a bike is that it feels just as good when you're grown up as it did when you weren't.

THE LAZY CYCLIST
Pace yourself

If you're just about to embark on a life on two wheels, be sure to ease yourself into it. That way you're much more likely to enjoy it and stick with it, rather than end up red-faced and frustrated, with aching muscles.

• Cycle at a leisurely pace rather than racing along with the Lycra clan. You'll enjoy the ride and will arrive at your destination fully composed, without any uncomfortable sweat patches. Choose a 'sit up and beg' bike that actually makes it hard to go fast, and relish the joy of style over speed.

• If you haven't cycled for a while, start off by doing a few laps of your local park, then graduate to short routes that you know, such as to the local shops or café.

• If your journey to work seems a little daunting, you could first cycle to your nearest bus stop or train station and do the rest of the journey by public transport. I still do this frequently, especially when reading a particularly good book. Just make sure you lock your bike up securely. You can gradually increase the distance of the cycle ride, and travel fewer stops on the bus or train.

• The worst thing you can do is force yourself to cycle when you're not in the mood, especially when you're just starting out. If you have a shocking hangover or your legs are stiff, give yourself a break. Cycle because you want to, not because you think you should.

'The bicycle is the most civilized conveyance known to man.'
Iris Murdoch, British writer, 1919–99

How to . . .
Find a bike you like

So you've decided to buy a bike. Great idea! The good news is that, in the middle of a modern cycling boom, there is a broader range of women's bikes available than ever before. But all this choice can be a little overwhelming, especially if you've not been in the saddle for a while. This chapter can help you find the best bike for you.

Firstly, my advice is to buy a bike you like. If you're happy with the way your bike looks and feels to ride, you will use it more. So, although you may be tempted to resurrect that old mountain bike you got for your 12th birthday which is rusting away in your parents' garage, I wouldn't advise it. Sell it on eBay and put the money towards a bike for the woman you've become, not the girl you were.

The first step – before you even enter a bike shop – is to think carefully about what you'll be using the bike for. Here's a little questionnaire to get you started. Simply ask yourself these questions, then look at the bike types on the following pages to see which bike rings most of your bells:

- Are you looking for a general 'run-around' – for a local commute, shopping or the school run?
- Are you just starting out, having not ridden for a while?
- Are you doing a long, regular commute and will you want to pick up some speed?
- Are you planning to enter races or long rides?
- Do you want to cycle at a leisurely pace and remain sweat free?
- Do you have hills to climb on your journey?
- Do you need to cart a lot of stuff around, including kids?
- Do you need to carry the bicycle upstairs to store it in your flat?
- Will you be cycling off-road?

The Bike Type Selector

	UTILITY	CITY HYBRID	SPORT HYBRID	ROAD BIKE	MOUNTAIN	FOLDER	ELECTRIC
RUN-AROUND	OOO	OOO	OO	O	OO	OOO	OOO
STARTING OUT	OOO	OOO	OO	O	OO	OOO	OOO
LONG COMMUTE	O	OO	OOO	OOO	OO	OO	OOO
LONGER RIDES	O	OO	OOO	OOO	OO	OO	cheating
LEISURELY PACE	OOO	OO	O	O	OO	OOO	OOO
HILLS	O	OO	OOO	OOO	OOO	OO	OOO
CARRYING STUFF	OOO	OOO	OO	O	OO	OO	OOO
CARRY BIKE	O	OO	OOO	OOO	OO	OOO	O
CYCLING OFF-ROAD	O	OO	O	O	OOO	OO	O

O = not ideal   OO = OK   OOO = get cycling!

A word of warning: bike brands, shops and online stores often use different terminology from one another when talking about bike 'types'. While mountain bikes and road bikes are pretty straightforward, the confusion arises when talking about bikes for general use. One shop's 'hybrid' is another shop's 'city bike', which is another shop's 'leisure bike'. This is because there has been a huge development in these types of bike in recent years and the definitions are still hazy. Just be sure the bike you like has all the elements you need for the type of cycling you'll be doing. Make sure you take a look at the illustration of each bike on the following pages. This will help you recognize certain features. I won't bleat on about technical details and it doesn't matter if you don't know your axle from your crank set, but it is really useful to understand how things like the weight of the bike or the shape of its handlebars, for example, affect its usability.

UTILITY BIKES

Brands: Pashley, Gazelle, Raleigh, Bobbin Bicycles, Velorbis, Dawes, Linus, Electra, Beg Bicycles, Creme, Viva, Schwinn.

There are many names used to describe this type of bike, including Dutch, sit-up-and-beg, traditional, town, leisure, classic and heritage – and while all are valid and describe the bike well, the one I'm going to stick with is utility.

This type of bike evolved when cycling went from being a hobby for the upper classes to a dependable mode of transport for all, in the early 1900s. It's often thought of as a Dutch bike, since this type of bike has remained commonplace in Holland while almost disappearing in other countries (the Dutch call them *Omafiets* meaning Grandma's bike). But the design originates from England and they were very much the 'people's nag' in the UK, Germany and Japan until they were widely usurped by the car.

But the good news is that, as utility cycling makes a comeback, so does this attractive style of bike. Many bike brands have seen the potential for resurrecting this sturdy yet stylish bicycle and there are plenty of new-wave utility bikes out there that combine authentic vintage flair with modern technical design.

Handlebars and cycling position

The key characteristic of this bike type is the handlebars. They are positioned higher than the saddle and curve around towards your body so you don't have to reach forward to hold them. This puts you in a more upright and comfortable – not to mention ladylike – position than that of a regular hybrid bike. The position is often known as 'sit up and beg' or, in China, 'holding the bed pan': strangely derogatory phrases for a posture that most riders – me included – say feels highly sophisticated. It's also worth noting that there are varying degrees of sit-up-and-beg-ness. Traditional Dutch brands may have handlebars much higher and wider than modern versions from UK or US manufacturers.

Frame, wheels and gears

Men's frames are a sturdy, symmetrical triangle whereas women's frames have a low curved top tube, a feature that is designed for practicality – jolly useful for dismounting with dignity – but also adds softness and femininity to the bike's shape. Utility frames are usually steel, which absorbs shock and ensures a smoother ride but is heavier than aluminium, so carrying the bike upstairs can leave you far more exhausted than riding it ever will.

Wheels are usually 26 or 28 inches in diameter with tough, hard-wearing tyres, wider than those on road bikes but not as chunky as mountain bike tyres.

Utility bikes often have a hub gear system, which means the gears are super-simple to use and look after. The gear and chain system are covered, so you hardly notice they're there and you change gear with a hand lever, often on the right handlebar. Gears usually range from three to seven speeds – great on flats but not an ideal ride if you are pedalling up the Pyrenees anytime soon.

Peripherals

- Mudguards to protect you and innocent passers-by from mud splats
- Sturdy rear rack to accommodate panniers or child seats
- Basket on the front (or ample space to attach one)
- Some brands come with internal dynamo lights, permanently attached and powered by your pedalling
- Kickstand

The test ride

When I first tried out a utility bike, the upright cycling position felt very strange but I soon began to enjoy the comfort and the feeling of sophistication. The cycling position encourages you to cycle at a leisurely

pace so you rarely work up a sweat, and it puts very little pressure on your arms and shoulders, making it easy to sustain. The upright position also ensures you can see traffic clearly and traffic can see you. I love this style of bike for cruising around town and I always smile when I see someone riding one – they just exude a certain elegance. They are great bikes for piling up with shopping, kids or picnic gear but they are heavy units – not great for when you want to pick up pace on a longer ride, climb a hill or carry the bike for any distance.

HYBRIDS

Brands: Specialized, Ridgeback, Charge, Giant, tokyobike, Cannondale, Peugeot, Raleigh, Fuji.

The original concept of a 'hybrid' is a bike that combines characteristics from a road bike and mountain bike. This results in a versatile, reliable bike that can be sold to the mass market. However, it's important to note that, these days, there are a wide range of hybrids and they don't always stick to the original concept. Some are much closer to road bikes for those who like a fast-tracked commute and others add characteristics from the utility bike into the mix and work best for general cycling about town. Ultimately, any bike that is not a mountain bike or a road bike will often be thrown into the hybrid category.

CITY HYBRIDS/CITY BIKES

This is a good all-rounder suited to urban cycling, and as a result usually called a city bike, commuter or city hybrid. You will be able to pick up pace on this type of bike, but will also feel comfortable going at a slower rate. In the past, hybrids have been somewhat dull-looking bicycles but fortunately there are some much snazzier models about these days.

Handlebars and cycling position

The handlebars are usually flat, but can be slightly swept back, and are often positioned higher than the saddle. As a result, the rider has a happy medium: not having to lean forward as much as with a road bike but not as upright as on a utility bike, making the city hybrid a familiar riding style if you've not been in the saddle since school.

Frame, wheels and gears

Women's frames generally have a top tube that is straight but slanted downwards towards the seat to allow easier mounting and dismounting. The wheel size is usually 26 or 28 inches in diameter, while tyres are somewhere between chunky, thick mountain bike tyres and those of the streamlined road bike, so you can cope with lumps and bumps and avoid punctures, but still achieve speed. City hybrids usually have around eight gears, so you can tackle hills and vary your speed easily without getting baffled by complicated gear systems. They are often derailleur gears, which need oiling and cleaning from time to time. See *Look after your bike*, p74.

Peripherals

Some city hybrids may have mudguards and rear racks and even baskets, again adopting more of the characteristics of utility bikes than road or mountain bikes.

The test ride

Having ridden a utility bike for a few years now, I recently fell in love with a new kid on the block: a city hybrid from Japanese company tokyobike. Its 1950s retro styling drew me into the shop in Shoreditch, London, and before I knew it I was test-riding this nippy little number, right out of the shop and all the way home. I found the extra speed I could get on this bike completely addictive but was also glad of its swept-back handlebars so I could pootle comfortably too. It's a seven-speed with derailleur gears, so I've had to clean and oil the chain a few times but the gears are easy to adjust by twisting the shifter on the right handlebar. I also love the lightness and slimness of this bike compared with my utility bike – I can easily bring it in and out of my flat, which is an added perk in the mornings. It doesn't get the adoring looks that my Pashley did but it gives me more of a rush to ride.

SPORTS HYBRIDS

If you want to go for something a little racier than a regular hybrid but you're not quite ready for the Tour de France yet, you could try a sports hybrid. At the other end of the hybrid scale, these bikes start to take on more of the characteristics of a road bike – lighter frame, thinner tyres – but they still have flat handlebars and perhaps a less hefty price tag. Sports hybrids are ideal if you're a confident cyclist and you are keen to embrace a more energetic style of cycling with longer rides and races on smooth roads.

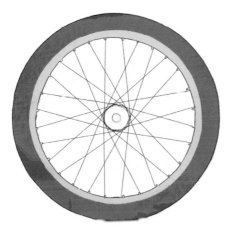

ROAD BIKES (RACERS)

Brands: Trek, Specialized, Bianchi, Scott, Eddy Merckx, Cannondale.

I find the term 'road bike' a little misleading: road bikes are not just bikes made to go on roads; they are bikes designed to go fast on smooth roads. This type of bike is also widely known as a racer or racing bike. I love the vintage-style racers with their simple lines, cool paintwork and leather-bound handlebars and saddles.

Handlebars and cycling position

Road bikes have drop handlebars – the ones that curve downwards. This allows the rider to take different positions to suit the terrain: holding the top of the handlebars is better for hill climbs, while placing your hands at the bottom gives a more aerodynamic position for picking up speed.

Frame, wheels and gears

Frames are lightweight, made of aluminium or carbon fibre; women's frames may have a very slightly slanted top tube but not always. Road-bike wheels are usually larger than those of women's mountain bikes or hybrids, at around 28 inches (confusingly, road-bike tyres are often called 700c, an old term that has stuck, the 'c' being to do with the type of rims the tyre was compatible with). Tyres are also thinner and have a higher PSI, meaning they will be harder when fully pumped up. This is what makes them faster – they have less contact with the ground than a wider, softer tyre that flattens more as it hits the ground. This flattening is called 'rolling resistance', and thin road-bike tyres have less of it, so they roll much faster. Road bikes have in the region of 16 to 24 gears, making it easier to tackle hills and hit optimum speeds.

Peripherals

The aim of a road bike is to be as streamlined as possible, so the only peripherals that feature are cleats or straps on the pedals to secure your feet in and help you go faster, and possibly also a water bottle cage so you can keep hydrated while riding. If you want a road bike that's more suited to taking luggage, you might want to look at a touring bike. Touring bikes have

similar performance to road bikes but are more robust and are designed to take luggage for long trips.

The test ride

I find the ride vastly different from what I'm used to. The forward-leaning position felt strenuous on my arms, shoulders and neck, and I was compelled to put more power into my pedalling. Although the speed is exhilarating, when slowing down to tackle a roundabout, I wobbled and felt vulnerable. A certain level of skill and fitness is required to ride a road bike but I have spoken to many women who have mastered the skill and claim they would never go back.

'I need a man like a fish needs a bicycle.'
Irina Dunn, Australian social activist, 1970

MOUNTAIN BIKES

Brands: Marin, GT, Kona, Felt Bicycles, Specialized, Trek, Giant, Mongoose.

The mountain bike phenomenon exploded in the 1980s launching these chunky little bikes far and wide, well beyond the mountains and into millions of suburban family garages. I owned one throughout my adolescence – all the kids on my street had them and we had a whale of a time splashing through puddles and racing around in the fields out the back. Although designed for off-road riding, mountain bikes (or MTBs) can make tough and agile commuting bikes.

Handlebars and cycling position

Handlebars are flat, giving a secure sports cycling position, but they are not as low as on a racer.

Frame, wheels and gears

Frames are compact and robust; women's models often having a slightly slanted top tube. Wheels are typically 26 inches in diameter and tyres wide and chunky for extra grip on uneven surfaces. Mountain bikes usually have lots of gears, around 20 to 30 speeds, to cater for the varying terrains and gradients involved in the sport.

Peripherals

Probably the bike with the least add-ons. No need for mudguards: if you are a serious mountain biker, getting splatted with mud is part of the fun. They won't come with baskets or racks, as these would be cumbersome and jangle or rattle on rough terrain, but if you are using an MTB for your commute you could fit a rear rack.

The test ride

Not the most elegant bike of the bunch but I have to say getting back on an MTB was fun! The suspension and chunky wheels allowed me to conquer large kerbs and potholes without getting off the bike, and it was great for cycling along gritty patches. They can be heavy to move around and you won't achieve any great speed, but an MTB is a perfect all-rounder bike if you like getting off-road at the weekends.

FOLDING BIKES

Brands: Brompton, Dahon, Mezzo, Raleigh.

Folders can make ideal
commuting companions as they
can be folded away to take
on buses or trains, and can be
brought along to the office,
theatre, pub or wherever it is
you're heading.

Handlebars and cycling position

Some have higher handlebars than others,
so the position can vary, but they are often
designed for comfort and usually provide
a fairly relaxed, upright ride.

Frame, wheels and gears

The frames are the same for men and
women but they are small and low so there's
no problem with mounting and dismounting.
The wheels are also small, which can be a
great advantage for city cycling as you can
get going much quicker after stopping in
traffic or at the lights. The folding mechanism
will vary from brand to brand but usually
there is a hinged join on the frame that
allows it to fold and the wheels can be
swivelled and clicked into place to form
a neat, compact bicycle package. Gears
typically range from two to ten speeds.

Peripherals

Peripherals can be tricky as they may
hinder the folding process. But brands like
Brompton recognize that commuters need
to carry things and have designed a special
bag that fits at the front when the bike
is unfolded.

The test ride

I went to Brompton HQ to test-ride a bright
pink beauty of a folder, hot off the factory
floor. It was a dream to ride: the small wheels
were nippy and agile, and there was no sense
of going slower than you would on a regular
bike. It was comfortable to ride and pretty
good at hills. The only problem I had was
when I dismounted and tried to remember
how to fold it. I had been given a tutorial but
was foggy on the details and needed some
practice until I got it right. Nevertheless, on
the whole I was very taken with this clever
little bike and loved the way it brightened up
my hall while taking up very little space.

Buying tip

Prices vary from £100 to over £1,000, but I
would be very wary of the cheaper models.
A lot goes into making these bikes, as they
have to be engineered to fold as well as ride,
and being able to produce a durable, safe
folder for £100 seems a little too good to be
true. So, if you fancy folding, do some sniffing
around and test-ride before you buy.

Miki Yamanouchi, London, UK

My Bike Friday Pocket Sport was made in Oregon, USA. It's an ultimate all-in-one versatile bike for me. You can take it on long tours and it folds when needed – say, in a restaurant where you don't feel safe to lock it outside. The 20-inch wheels are perfect for my body size and it's very easy to handle yet it covers a good distance with certain speed. Drop handlebars also give you freedom to change your position to prevent stiffness and adapt to road conditions. Another bike I have is a smaller vintage Moulton mini, which I call my 'pub bike'. With this I don't get too nervous locking it outside, anytime, anywhere.

The Japanese cycle scene is now in a huge transition and has a growing interest in good-quality bikes instead of poorly made, cheap ones. Small-wheel folding bikes are extremely popular due to limited living space.

ELECTRIC BIKES

Brands: B'TWIN, Spencer Ivy, Ave, EcoBike, Powacycle, Easy Motion, Prodeco, Moustache.

Electric bikes have been looked down on in the past as uncool traitors to pedal power. I remember my dad coming home with one once – my siblings and I, all unforgiving teenagers at the time, disapproved – and it spent a lot more time in the shed than it did on the road. But electric bikes are finally getting some recognition – even Prince Charles and Leonardo DiCaprio are fans. So, if you like the idea of an electrical push up the hills, why not give one a whirl?

The electrical element has been much improved and many new bikes are modelled on attractive utility-bike designs. There are two main types of electric bike:

- Pedelec – The pedelec has a small motor that assists you as you cycle and will cut out when you stop cycling or reach a certain speed. Generally they don't go over 25 miles per hour and are classified as regular bicycles rather than mopeds.

- Twist and go – The motor can be activated by a throttle on the handlebar so you don't need to pedal to move. These are classified as mopeds, so different rules apply when riding these on the roads.

Handlebars and cycling position

Technically, an electric bike can be any bike with a motor but the most common for commuters are based on traditional or city-bike designs so cycling position is upright and comfortable.

Frame, wheels and gears

Frames and wheels tend to be sturdy and similar to those of utility or city bikes. The battery and motor are housed in a box between the seat tube and the rear wheel. The motor attaches to the rear wheel hub, to power the bike. The battery can be removed and charged by a household mains socket. Electric bikes have gears and brakes. Gears may vary but, for commuter models, six to eight speeds is standard.

Peripherals

You can now get electric bikes with a myriad of peripherals: dynamo lights, integrated frame lock, rear rack, basket, kickstand, mudguards. Just be aware that with all these extras and the motor/battery it will be a heavy bike and getting it upstairs to a flat is not going to be practical – unless you fancy a strenuous physical challenge to counteract the easier ride.

The test ride

Like many cyclists, I am not quite convinced about electric bikes, as pedal power serves me perfectly well. But, with a 'don't knock it till you've tried it' attitude, I climbed aboard a very attractive 'e-bike' from French brand Moustache to see if I could be converted. Just one quick rotation of the pedals and I feel that magic push. The instant acceleration is a shock, but a good one, and soon I am having fun, amazed at how fast I am going and itching to try a hill. It's easy-peasy to use – the motor just kicks in as you cycle and you can up the amount of 'push' by pressing a button on the left handlebar grip. While I don't feel the need to replace my old-school bicycle and go electric, I now understand how these very clever bikes could help get swathes more people into cycling, as they are easy and fun.

ALTERNATIVE RIDES

TANDEM RIDERS

Brands: Dawes, Circe Cycles, Canondale, Trek, Claud Butler.

Not the most practical mode of transport for the daily commute (unless you are extremely close to a colleague), but tandems can be great fun for weekend trips and touring. They are also handy for getting older children around and they don't have to be limited to two saddles: you can get tandems for three or four (the word tandem does not actually mean 'two'; it refers to the seating arrangement with one person behind another). They may cost more than a regular bike, but prices are not through the roof. Styles do differ depending on function, with more slender models for racing and touring and studier models for leisure cycling.

The test ride

The tricky first step of riding a tandem is learning how to start and stop, as you need to be synchronized with your partner – but you soon get the knack. The person who goes up front is called the captain and they have full control of the steering and braking, while the person who goes behind (the stoker) takes a more subservient role and just pedals. I started as the stoker and was instantly freaked out by the lack of control and kept reaching for my non-existent brakes. Call me a control freak, but I was much happier in the captain position. You're not going to go unnoticed on a tandem and, as long as there are no arguments about who's in charge, it can be heaps of fun.

CRUISERS

Cruisers came on the market in the US after the great depression in the 1930s. Bike manufacturers looking for a new angle designed them to look like motorcycles to appeal to the youth market. They enjoyed popularity until the 1950s and have had a resurgence in recent years with many an LA celebrity being spotted on one. They have chunky frames and big tyres, known as balloon tyres, swept-back handlebars and a basket up front for your beach gear.

The test ride

Possibly the most relaxed ride I've ever had. The cycling position is super comfy and the bike is heavy, which means you can't do anything too adventurous on it. Cycling slowly on a flat path with the wind blowing in your hair is the ideal way to ride on a cruiser.

FIXED-GEAR BIKE

If you have ever wondered what the difference between a single-speed and a fixed-gear bike is, I will clear it up for you now. Both only have one gear but on a single-speed bike you can coast or freewheel, while with a fixed-gear bike you cannot – if you stop pedalling the bike will brake to a stop. Many fixies have something called a flip-flop hub that enables you to switch between the two.

But fixed-gear bikes seem to be about so much more than the technical detail – they have created a burgeoning subculture of hipsters in cities all over the world and are regarded by many to be the ultimate cool set of wheels.

The test ride

The first thing that strikes me is how slim and light my Charge Plug bike is. There's a single-speed cog on one side and a fixed-gear cog on the other, so you can switch by taking the wheel off and flipping it round. As a single speed, it's a lovely ride (and I feel rather cool), making me question if gears are really necessary. Starting off in the fixed gear takes some getting used to as you can't play around with the pedals to line them up. It's also strange when you try to stop cycling but the pedals keep on rotating. I soon get the hang of adjusting my pedalling speed and am able to come to a graceful stop. This bike would not work for me every day but it was fun, and in another life I might fancy going fixed.

BESPOKE BIKES

Not happy with any of the bikes on offer in your bike shop? Then why not design your own? There has been a rise in companies catering for the style-savvy cycling brigade who want to put an individual stamp on their bikes. Bespoke bikes not only allow you to get a bike that fits perfectly, but you can also choose specific colours for your frame, saddle and even your chain.

'Get a bicycle. You will certainly not regret it, if you live.'
Mark Twain, *Taming the Bicycle,* 1884

Melissa Davies, San Francisco, USA
Blog: bikepretty.com

I own three bikes. My favourite is a bamboo single-speed with a belt-drive instead of a chain. I built the frame myself at the now-closed San Francisco Bamboo Bike Studio. The bamboo is such a conversation starter. A lot of people ask me, 'Who made that for you?' and I get to say, 'I made it myself!' Since the belt-drive doesn't use any grease, I don't worry about getting chain marks on my shoes and stockings. That makes it the ultimate fashion bike.

Amanda Mills, Milwaukee, Wisconsin, USA

I ride a 1973 Schwinn Voyager. It was originally a 21-speed but I rebuilt it into a fixed-gear for commuting. I love my bike because I rebuilt it with my own two hands. It has this lovely original chrome paint job that just flashes! I have green glitter and teal deep-vs, a handmade top-tube cover, and shiny streamers that I got at a local bike shop. This bike is a part of me and my style, just like the clothes I wear. The bike fits me like a glove and we're pretty inseparable in the summertime.

SECOND-HAND BIKES WITH STYLE

If you're a vintage lover on a budget, then opting for a second-hand bike could be a great way to find your perfect steed. Not only do they have retro charm, but you can get some incredibly well-built, reliable bikes for under £100. Try and go for a bike built between the 1950s and 1980s. This is seen as a golden era – a large volume of high-quality women's bikes were manufactured during this period and, unlike bikes from the 1920s and 1930s, you can still get the components for them, should they need repairing.

What to look out for

- Raleigh bicycles
  Vintage Raleigh bikes not only look wonderful but really can stand the test of time with strong steel frames and weatherproof gearing systems. Raleigh was the leading bike manufacturer for many years and they were shipped all over the world. My favourites are the cute-as-a-button Raleigh shoppers.

- Check the frame is not bent or cracked
  While superficial marks add character, a bike with a seriously damaged frame is not worth buying and a crack could lead to it snapping completely. Look closely at the whole of the frame, especially where the tubes join together.

- Car boot sales
  These are a great way to find a real vintage nugget and, unlike buying online, you can try before you buy.

- Mixte frame
  This style of frame originates from France and is a sturdier alternative to a step-through frame. The slanted top tube extends all the way back to the rear axle (i.e. the centre of the back wheel) instead of stopping at the seat tube. Mixte frames have an attractive and durable geometry so are a great choice for a second-hand bike. Brands to look out for are Peugeot, Mercier and Gitane.

With a vintage bike, there is, of course, a risk that there will be technical problems. If you're buying online, try to have a thorough conversation with the seller about the condition of the bike or, if they are local, arrange a viewing first. Ask about all the key components: frame, wheels, brakes and gears, and check that all parts can be easily repaired and replaced. Factor in the extra cost you will pay for postage, assembling and servicing if you are not a whizz with mechanics, to make sure you won't be out of pocket.

Before you buy, take a look at the M check in *Maintain your bike* (p74) as a starting point for assessing the bike. Fixing up an old bike can be fun and rewarding if your heart is in it. But if you don't want to sign up to a Sunday project, find a bike shop that reconditions old bikes so you can get a tip-top vintage charmer without getting your hands dirty.

WHAT SIZE DO I NEED?

With the exception of folders,
bikes are measured by frame size,
which is the length of the seat tube.

Take a look at the chart below for a standard
women's utility bike. The sizes may differ
from brand to brand but the pattern will
be similar. The size of the bike frame should
correspond to your height and inside leg
measurement. Good bike shops will size you
up and try you with the size they think is right.

FRAME SIZE	RIDER HEIGHT	INSIDE LEG
SMALL (17")	4'11"–5'3"	26"–29"
MEDIUM (19")	5'3"–5'6"	29"–32"
LARGE (21")	5'6"–5'9"	32"–35"

Once you've decided on the frame size,
there is some fine tuning to be done:

Saddle

Most seat posts can be adjusted to ensure
you get the saddle at the perfect height for
the best cycling position. The best way to
get this right is to sit evenly on your saddle
with one pedal in the downwards position.
With the arch of your foot on the pedal, you
should be able to get your leg completely
straight. When you are in motion, this means
your leg will be very nearly straight on the
downward stroke. If your saddle is too low
and your knees remain bent as you cycle,
it will make cycling harder work and could
even damage your knees. If your saddle is

too high, you will struggle to keep your feet
on the pedals and could lose control. Once
you think you've got it right, just check that
you can stop and dismount easily – a high
saddle may feel good for cycling but could
make it tricky to stop.

Handlebars

Many bikes allow you to adjust the height
of the handlebars but some do not – so
be sure to check before you buy. There are
no fixed rules when it comes to handlebar
position, as personal preference plays a big
part. But you want to ensure that you can
reach them easily and you don't have to
stretch too far forward. If you are not quite
certain what feels right at the beginning,
ensure that you buy a bike with adjustable
handlebars so you can play around with
them. You can also move the saddle forward
or back on the rods that attach it to the seat
post, so you can adjust your distance to the
handlebars as well.

A bike fitting

If you are investing in a road bike and want
to be sure you've got your position just
perfect, you could sign up for a professional
bike fitting. Your position and style of riding
will be analyzed by an expert, and minor
tweaks will be made to improve your
performance and to prevent aches and pains
as much as possible. Expect to pay your way,
though – this kind of expert knowledge
doesn't come for free.

BEFORE YOU BUY

Take a test ride

Test-riding a few bikes before you make the big decision is vital, and any bike shop that won't accommodate this is not worth its salt. You need to get a buzz from your bike as well as feeling comfortable, safe and, of course, ensuring that all your requirements are met.

Don't forget that special something

While it is important to consider the practicalities when buying a bike, don't be afraid to be swayed by a certain *je ne sais quoi*. If that canary-yellow frame makes you squeal with delight every time you hop aboard, your love affair with cycling will blossom. Aesthetic considerations should not be dismissed in favour of technical prowess.

PROFILE
Sian Emmison, London, founder
of Bobbin Bicycles
Website: bobbinbikes.co.uk/
wordpress

Sian and Tom set up Bobbin Bicycles in
2006. They started out with a shop in East
London that sold stylish, traditional bikes
to a growing breed of urban cyclists. They
focused on what the customer wanted, with
a policy to spend at least an hour with each
prospective buyer to ensure the bike was the
right match. Realizing the growing demand
for stylish town bikes, they then went on to
manufacture their own, launching the Bobbin
brand in 2010. Today, their beautiful bicycles
are sold all over the world.

What advice would you give to people when first buying a bike?
People are often nervous and out of their
comfort zone when buying a bike for the
first time. The key is to welcome them,
get them chatting and make them feel at
ease. We would start by asking them what
type of cycling they do or want to do, and
what they want from the bike.

Would you advise buying a bike in person from a shop or is it OK to buy online?
You can figure out the size you need and
buy online, but nothing beats having a go and
getting a feel for it. It's going to be your best
mate. The other bonus of buying from a shop
is that they will often offer you a free service
3–4 weeks after you buy. When you first ride a
bike, things move and loosen up so it's a really
good idea to get it checked out at this juncture.

What types of saddle are most comfortable?
On a sit-up-and-beg bike you are sitting
square on the saddle, so it's a certain style
specific for that position, but it may not work
on a racer. We use sprung saddles. They
absorb the shock much better. We also use
steel frames. Steel absorbs shock. If you're on
an aluminium bike, it will feel lighter but will
also feel hollow and the vibrations will come
up through your arms and make for a much
shakier ride.

One last piece of advice?
People often buy a bike based on what
it looks like and it's fine to go for a bike
because you fall in love with it, but it's
important that it's going to do what you
want it to do, so you need to know about
the components or have someone explain
them in a way that makes sense.

3

How to . . .
Accessorize your ride

Once you are sorted with a set of wheels the next step is accessories. You don't need to have every gadget going but there are a few staples that will make your life by bike much easier and much safer. Shopping for bike accessories might seem like a necessary evil, but in today's bicycle-savvy times it can actually be much more fun than you might think.

When I first started cycling as an adult, I was frustrated beyond belief by the bland and positively dorky bike accessories on offer. I began a one-woman crusade to find stylish cycling accessories – and I was so inspired by the products I found and so keen to spread the word to other women that I started a business selling them. Cyclechic.co.uk was set up in 2008 and we still take great pride in seeking out and selling the very best accessories we can find to ladies who cycle – and like to look and feel good doing it.

It's all very well having a pretty basket but if it's a real pain to attach it or it's wobbly and unsafe when you ride, then it's not going to be helping you that much. So, my advice is to find accessories that are practical, safe and make you smile, and you'll soon be wondering how you ever cycled without them.

Useful accessories >>>

Helmet
Bell
D lock
Chain or cable lock
Saddle lock
Saddlebag
Pannier (single or double)
Basket or dog basket
Front and rear lights
Multi-tool
Reflectors
Reflective sash
Hand or floor pump
Water bottle
Waterproof jacket/cape
Gloves

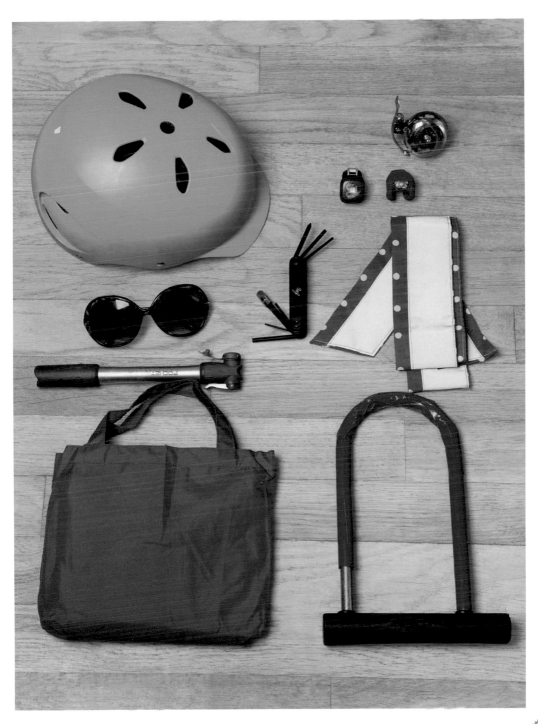

LOCK IT UP

Brands: Abus, Kryptonite, Squire and OnGuard.

A good lock is essential if you plan on parking your bike anywhere that isn't 100 per cent secure. Now, when it comes to a lock, we can let style slide. You don't have to wear it and its duty is to guard your bike and keep thieves at bay, so security is the number one priority.

Unfortunately, a determined thief with a sophisticated tool kit can break any lock, given time, so all you can do is make it as hard for them as possible.

My advice is to go for a good, strong D lock. This is basically an oversized padlock. It comprises a metal U shape (the shackle) that connects into a bar with a lock mechanism inside (the barrel), and it locks and unlocks with a key.

What to look for in a D lock

Sold Secure rating: Sold Secure is a British organization that tests locks. Locks that make the grade are awarded with a Bronze, Silver or Gold level of security, based on the time it takes to break into them, with Bronze taking the shortest time and Gold the longest (i.e. the most secure). Outside the UK, look for ratings from Stichting ART in the Netherlands, SFF in Sweden and VDS in Germany.

Length of the U: You need to ensure the U is long enough to allow you to fit it around the object you are locking it to but, at the same time, if it's too long, thieves can use the space to get more leverage. You will not be locking the bike in the same place every time so, when identifying parking spots, it's worth keeping in mind how much girth you need. If you are just using a D lock and no additional lock, you may want to go for a longer U so you can try to lock the front wheel and the frame.

Mounting bracket: D locks are heavy so a good idea is to buy one that comes with a mounting bracket or Velcro straps that attach the lock to your bike frame. The bike then carries your lock safely while you're riding so you don't have to lug it around in a bag. If your lock does not have mounting brackets, a bike basket is a handy place to keep it – but just check the basket is strong enough to take the weight.

Rubber casing: Try to get a D lock with a rubber casing to prevent it chipping the paint on your bike frame when you lock it.

Other types of lock

Cable locks: These come in a range of sizes and thicknesses, and are more flexible than D locks and often lighter. This makes them easier to transport, but they are also easier for thieves to cut with bolt cutters.

Chain locks: As you might imagine, these are simply chains that secure with a padlock. A chunky chain lock can be very hard to break; however, they can be heavy and cumbersome to carry. You can get chain locks that come with a sheath wrapped around them, to be worn around your hips like a belt, but the weight may become a drag after a while.

Folding locks: These are a relatively new type of lock. They have a link construction, so the lock extends out to be looped around the bike and bike stand, but then folds back into a compact shape when unlocked, making it much easier to store and carry. Some also come with a pouch that attaches the lock to the frame with Velcro.

Saddle locks: These can be useful if you have a nice expensive saddle that could be a target for thieves. A thin cable lock is a good idea to secure it to the seat post. If you have a quick-release saddle you could replace this with bolts – ask at your hardware store or bike shop if they have anti-theft bolts that need a special type of Allen key to open.

HELMETS

Brands: Bern, Sawako Furuno, Lazer, Yakkay.

You may think it strange but I have spent the last six years of my life borderline obsessed with bike helmets. It all started with disgust and shame at having to wear a very ugly, angular monstrosity when I first started to cycle to work. This led to a quest to find a stylish bike helmet that was safe and comfortable to wear. Since starting my business, I am pleased to say that I have found many helmets that have filled this brief, and I now have a personal wardrobe of helmets to rival the Queen's hat collection.

I have also had the pleasure of helping many a customer find the right helmet for her. When I first started Cyclechic women would come to my flat, try on helmets and leave with their head held much higher than when they arrived, having upon it a helmet that they actually liked.

'I enjoy a spin on my tandem bicycle. It is splendid to feel the wind blowing in my face and the springy motion of my iron steed.' Helen Keller, American deaf and blind political activist, 1880–1968

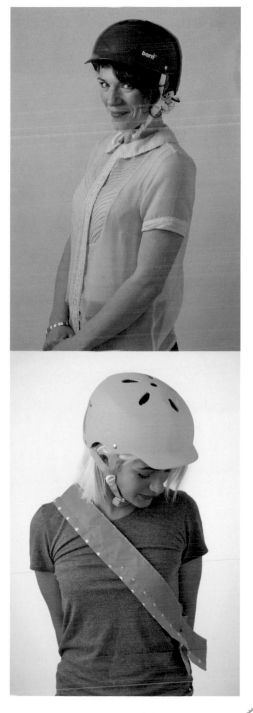

Jude Brosnan, London
Blog: ispeakbike.blogspot.co.uk

Hi, my name is Jude and I'm a helmetaholic. I have, over time, amassed quite a collection. In my defence, I do spend most of my time on my bike, wearing helmets. You wouldn't wear the same pair of shoes every day, would you? I like to customize my helmets and match them with my outfits. I have a bright pink one which I pimped with disco mirror squares and wore for a night ride to celebrate my 30th birthday. Another favourite is a sportier style that I have covered with a turban and added a brooch to. I love the vintage touch it adds to my outfits. And my current fave is a turquoise Bern helmet. At first I thought the colour may be too bright, but it seems to go with everything and people can see me for miles around.

To wear or not to wear: that is the question

Wearing a helmet is not compulsory (unless you live in Australia) but, if you are just starting out and have safety fears, it can be a huge boost to your confidence. I have spoken to many cyclists who feel very strongly about helmet-wearing and would never cycle without one, and also to others who have cycled helmet-free for years. The decision is up to you.

The major barrier that put me off cycling in a big city was the fear of sharing the road with traffic. Wearing a helmet, and getting some professional cycle training, helped me overcome this fear. I wear a helmet because it makes me feel more secure on my bike and gives me confidence, which means I am a calmer, more astute cyclist. It does not mean I take risks and I am not under any illusion that it's a magical solution preventing me from injury. It's quite simply that I feel safer and happier cycling on the road with a helmet than I do without.

My advice would be to have a dig around online and look at the arguments for and against. Cycle with one and then cycle without one, and make your own decision about what feels right for you.

Many of us have helmet hang-ups when we first start cycling. We don't want to ruin our street cred or our hair. Or maybe we just find them annoying and uncomfortable to wear. But if you get a comfortable helmet that looks good on, many of these hang-ups can be overcome. See *Cycle to work* (p168) for tips on how to combat helmet hair.

The science bit

Most bike helmets consist of a moulded plastic shell and a lining of EPS (expandable polystyrene), which is usually about an inch thick, covering the interior of the helmet, with gaps for the ventilation holes. It's this EPS that is the key safety feature, meaning that bike helmets pass international safety standards (CPSC, ASTM 2040, EN1077B and EN1078) and gain certification. The way it works is this: when your helmet impacts on a surface or object during a fall, the EPS foam absorbs the force before it hits your head. The reason that this type of material works so well is because it will crush on impact and won't bounce and send the force back to your head. Although there will be some impact of the foam on your head, the polystyrene absorbs the shock and prevents a more serious blow.

Types of helmet

As with buying a bike, it's a good idea to have a think about the type of cycling you

are going to be doing when considering what type of helmet you might need. If you're going to be cycling on a road bike and picking up speed, you will want a helmet that's lightweight and well ventilated, but if you're going to be leisurely cycling around town, you might not be so concerned about ventilation and want a helmet that fits in with your everyday wardrobe.

Standard bike helmets: These are based on a sporty style and are not particularly flattering but are usually low cost, light, well ventilated and do the job. Brands: Met, Giro, Bell.

Skate/BMX-style helmets: Skate-style helmets are more rounded than standard helmets, with subtler ventilation holes, and are often a good option when starting out. They are more flattering than the standard style, come in an array of colours and designs, and are usually reasonably priced. Brands: Bell, Bobbin, Giro, Bern, Pro-Tec.

Peaked helmets: The peaked style, patented by Bern, takes its influence from snowboarding and horseriding helmets. The reason most helmets do not flatter is because they stop abruptly at the front of your head and create a kind of mushroom effect. The peak prevents this and works much better with the natural shape of your head and face. Some come with the peak permanently attached but others have a removable peak, sometimes made of a light canvas fabric similar to that of a baseball cap.

The peak is not just a style feature, however; it's also great for keeping sun and rain out of your eyes. This makes cycling more comfortable but is also a huge safety plus point, as sun and rain in your eyes can distort your vision. These helmets may be slightly heavier than other styles and don't have as many ventilation holes as more sporty helmets but they are a great option for style and comfort. Brands: Bern, SAHN, Giro.

Fashion helmets: The main brand making waves with fashionable helmets that reflect modern style is Sawako Furuno. Helmets in her collection include croc leather, leopard print, floral and pretty Japanese graphics. Another popular fashion brand is Yakkay, which has designed a plain, smooth helmet base and various covers that can be fitted over the top to disguise the helmet as a hat. They have less ventilation than some other helmet types but are a wonderfully smart option for any cycling stylista, as you can change the hat-cover as often as you change your outfit.

Road helmets: These are much more technical and prices can go up to £170. They will be very well ventilated, very lightweight and designed with the aerodynamics of the rider in mind. Brands: Giro, Specialized, Scott.

Folding helmets: If you are fed up with carrying your helmet around off the bike, a fold-up helmet could be just the ticket. There are a few brands unfolding on to the market, but the best is Carrera as their helmets look pretty sleek and fold down to a third of the size to fit discreetly in your bag.

FITTING A HELMET

1. Measure up: The first step is to measure your head. Find a flexible tape measure and place it around the circumference of your head, pulling it taut. (The tape measure should be positioned as in the diagram below.) Most helmets will have size breakdowns measured in centimetres – see below for an example of a typical sizing table. Knowing your head measurement is a good place to start when trying on helmets and it will also make it possible to order your helmet online, as small local shops can have a limited range.

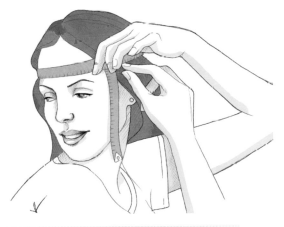

SIZE	MEASUREMENT
EXTRA SMALL	52–53.5 cm
SMALL	53.5–55.5 cm
MEDIUM	55.5 -57 cm
LARGE	57–59 cm
EXTRA LARGE	59–60.5 cm

2. Positioning: Once you've selected a helmet, push it down on your head, ensuring it sits level and does not tilt backwards or forwards. You may have an urge to tilt it back as you would a hat but this is not the correct position, and is not safe – so resist.

3. The perfect fit: The helmet should feel snug but not uncomfortably tight. Many helmets have some way to adjust the size slightly, from dials at the back to Velcro straps or even padded inserts. Now is the time to play around with any adjustable features and check your head is getting a nice gentle hug, and you don't feel like you're balancing a fruit bowl on it.

4. Strap up: The next step is to tighten the chin strap. The 'Y' shape should fit just underneath your ears. The strap needs to be tight enough to keep your helmet secure on your head but not so tight that it's cutting off your air supply. A good trick is to ensure you can fit one finger between your chin and the strap, once tightened.

5. The wobble test: Finally, with your helmet secure and the straps fastened, wobble your head from side to side. If the helmet moves, it's too big or you need to readjust. If it does not wobble, keep the helmet on for five minutes. If it's pressing or hurting and you can't wait to get it off – it's too small. If you are wobble and headache free – well done, you got yourself the perfect fit.

BAGS, BASKETS AND PANNIERS

I very rarely go anywhere on my bike without having stuff to take with me – whether it's my laptop, a few groceries, my yoga gear or bargains I've picked up from a car boot sale, there's always something to carry. As many bikes don't come with built-in racks or luggage provision, it's often presumed that carrying stuff while cycling makes for an awkward ride. In fact, the opposite is true – with the right accessories you can carry far more by bike than you can on foot. So don't struggle with a bulky rucksack or balance your bags precariously over the handlebars, get your luggage set-up sorted and you'll never look back.

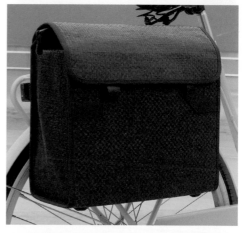

BAGS

Brands: Bagaboo, Timbuk2, Blind Chic, Brooks, Michaux, Deuter, Carradice, Bramble and Mr Twigg, Good Ordering, Linus, Pashley, Cyclodelic.

Cycling-specific bags

There are many types of bag designed especially to be worn when cycling and you may find these are the most practical option

if you have quite a bit of kit to carry around. Designs usually take into account wearability, weatherproofing, ventilation and visibility – and will keep you well balanced when riding. From classic leather rucksacks to street-style messenger bags, there are some nice-looking cycle specific bags around that will not be out of place once you've locked up and headed into the office, pub or café.

Messenger bags: Courier-style messenger bags, designed especially for cycling, usually have a large strap that goes across your chest and shoulders, and may have a waist strap to keep the bag securely on your back. They are often pretty roomy and can have a special space for your laptop.

Rucksacks: A general rucksack will work fine on a bike but cycle-specific backpacks may have the addition of a waist strap and are designed to sit comfortably when cycling. They may also have additional features, like loops to attach lights and zip-up pockets galore.

Handlebar bags: These strap on to your handlebars, usually with a quick-release mechanism or leather straps for the more classically styled. You can get some very cute handlebar bags that double up as shoulder bags when off the bike. Perfect for your day-to-day essentials.

And don't forget saddlebags: These attach to the saddle rails and/or the seat post and are ideal for carrying life's essentials. They tuck away neatly but can usually fit quite a bit inside, even a spare inner tube.

Handbags and glad rags

However, you don't have to choose a
bag designed specifically for cycling. Many
ordinary kinds of bag work well on the bike,
from small chain purses to large leather
satchels. The key is to find a bag that sits
comfortably and securely on your back while
you ride, and doesn't swing forward and get
in the way. A handbag is usually fine, as long
as it has a long shoulder strap so that it sits
diagonally across your body.

Handbags on bikes

If, try as you might, your beloved
handbag does not sit right when
you cycle, here are a few ideas:

Handbag hugger
This is a rack that attaches to
your handlebar stem and clasps
your handbag tight. Unlike a bike
basket, it sits on the inside of
your handlebars so your precious
belongings are never out of arm's
reach.

Bungees on the back
You can either use simple bungee
straps or an elasticated net that
clips on to the rear rack and
keeps your bag in place.

Basket cover
If you have a bike basket but
feel worried that someone might
swipe your handbag from it, then
this shower-cap-like cover could
be the solution. The Dorothy
cover is waterproof, elasticated
and tightens with a drawstring,
so it keeps your bag dry and
safe. They come in a nice range
of colours and have reflective
patches on, for night cycling.

WITH BELLS ON

It's an international legal requirement to have a bell on your bike, and a lot of new bikes will come with one already fitted. I find I mostly use mine for letting pedestrians know I'm there on shared paths, and it's a good idea to ding your bell just before you go under a bridge or subway, when you can't see or be seen from the other end.

If your bike doesn't already have a bell, they're easy enough to attach. Most come with a metal bracket and two screws; more modern bells may attach with a plastic strap. When positioning the bell on the handlebar you want to be sure it's close enough to the handlebar grip so you can reach for it without taking your hand away. Bells usually go on the left, the opposite side to the gear lever or shifter. You can go for something very plain and functional or you can have a bit of fun and go for a patterned bell, like the Electra bells below, but, most importantly, it must be easy for you to use while riding and must make a good clear sound.

BASKETS

Brands: Basil, Bobbin, KLICKfix, Nantucket Bike Basket Co., Adie, Wald.

A basket can be a great addition to your bike. Whether you're piling it high with fresh veg and French sticks or, more realistically, throwing your bag in it on your way to work, a basket can be a practical choice that can add oodles of character and charm to your bike.

If your bike is currently basketless, do not fear; there are plenty of options to choose from. The best bikes for attaching baskets to are utility bikes or city hybrids, as the handlebars are higher so there is more space to fit one in.

Wicker

You can't beat a wicker basket on a bicycle for vintage style. The most common sort is D shaped but you can also get oval and rectangular. The reason bike baskets are often made of wicker is because it is strong and lightweight.

Plastic (wicker effect)

Wicker looks very pretty but, when left out in the rain, it can lose its colour, go mouldy and eventually rot. A more durable alternative is a plastic, wicker-effect basket. From a distance, you can't tell the difference and it will prove to be far more weatherproof (I won't tell if you don't).

Metal

Metal baskets can be sturdy, reliable and have an unassuming allure. Being a long-time wicker fan, I recently started using a Wald grocery basket, as it has a 1950s feel that suits my bike, and I have found it to be extremely accommodating. You can also get the no-nonsense wire mesh type of basket: not much to look at but strong and durable. Both types may rust over time, however, if left out in the rain.

How do they attach to the bike?

Small, simple wicker baskets have either two metal hooks that simply attach to the handlebars, or two leather straps that fasten with buckles. This type of wicker basket is very easy to take on and off, and works well for light loads. But, if overloaded, it may affect your steering, and it's also very easily pinched off the bike.

If you want to carry more weight, you might want to go for a basket that has a supporting bracket underneath it, which connects to the grooves in the bike fork down by the hub of the wheel. It may be an idea to have this fitted in a bike shop as you need to be sure the bracket is the right size to hold the basket firmly in place.

For a basket that's easy to attach yourself and also has strong support, try a brand like KLICKfix. All baskets come with a bracket specifically designed to attach easily to the handlebar stem or top of the frame – rather than the handlebars – so that the steering is not affected. The bracket also holds the basket a short distance from the bike so you don't have the issue of the basket squashing

the brake cables. They usually have a lock or quick release so you can detach the basket and take it shopping with you.

Dog baskets

Brands: TRIXIE, Pet Ego and Solvit Tagalong.

If you want to carry your pooch around on your bike, you will need a dog-specific basket. You could be taking a risk with a regular basket as it may not be able to take the weight or be designed for contents that can move around! You can get wicker dog baskets for both front and rear, some of which come with a fleecy lining and a cage that goes over the top to stop your dog leaping out. You can also get canvas bags and baskets that come with a mesh cover, specific brackets to connect them to the handlebars, and shoulder straps to carry when off the bike.

Three tips for cycling with dogs:

- Let your dog get used to the bike basket before you go out for a ride.
- Don't attach the lead to the dog's collar when riding – if he leaps out, he could hurt his neck.
- If your dog is too large for a front basket, try a basket that attaches to the rear rack, or even a trailer – you can get dog-specific bike trailers.

Things to watch out for with baskets

Don't overload
If you pile up your basket with too much shopping or a stack of books, you could find things topple out along the way. This could be both distressing and dangerous.

Don't leave your basket out in the rain
If you have to leave your bike outside, try to detach the basket and bring it inside to prevent it getting wet and moulding or rusting.

Baskets may affect steering and braking
If your basket is attached to the handlebars only, it may affect your steering and braking. Try to get your basket fitted at a bike shop to avoid this problem.

Basket bandits
If your handbag is exposed, there is a chance it could be swiped out of your basket if you get distracted. Try a basket cover or even secure your bag with a bungee strap, and make sure you don't lock up your bike and wander off, leaving your precious goods in your basket.

PANNIERS

Brands: Ortlieb, Altura, Linus, New Looxs, Basil, Bobbin.

Panniers are a wonderful way to carry your belongings safely and securely on your bicycle. All you need is a rear rack on the back of your bike. Again, many utility bikes and commuter bikes will already come with a rack in place. But if not, a rack can easily be attached to most bikes.

A rear rack sits over the rear wheel; it connects with two rods that bolt to grooves on the frame next to the rear axle. It then has a bracket or two arms that connect to the seat stay, on the frame. If you are unsure how to attach it, buy one in a shop and ask them to fit it for you. There are a wide range of racks on the market but a very basic design should take about 20 kilograms and will be fine for commuting and shopping; you may want to get a slightly more advanced model for carrying around lots of luggage.

Panniers went through a phase of being boring and boxy but there are now some great options out there. They are often made of a durable, waterproof PVC fabric and may have multiple pockets for all your different bits and bobs. If you want something hardwearing and weatherproof, look at brands like Ortlieb and Altura, who specialize in panniers that are fully waterproofed to cope with harsh conditions and close tightly to ensure not a drop of water can get in.

You can also get panniers that are geared towards the more style-savvy cyclist, made from nicely designed textiles, or single panniers that look like regular bags and satchels.

Double panniers

Double panniers straddle the rear rack and usually attach on with straps or buckles. They are ideal for cycling holidays and adventures when you need to carry lots of luggage. They can be fiddly to get off the bike, so may not be ideal for commuting or city use. However, if you are able to keep your bike indoors, you can leave them on the bike. Double panniers can take a good deal of weight and will balance it out evenly on either side if packed correctly.

'The bicycle is just as good company as most husbands and, when it gets old and shabby, a woman can dispose of it and get a new one without shocking the entire community.'
Ann Strong, *Minneapolis Tribune*, 1895

The single pannier (the Commuting Queen)

My recommendation for carrying your belongings easily with the least amount of hassle has to be the single pannier. At Cyclechic, single panniers are one of our biggest sellers, second only to helmets. A single pannier transformed my commute to work: having had problems attaching a sturdy basket and then having struggled with various bags, when I eventually got a rear rack and a single pannier, it was an instant hit. The pannier usually clips on to your rear rack with one simple movement and comes off just as easily – and it will have handles and often a shoulder strap, so once you take it off the bike it essentially becomes a normal bag.

If your pannier is for work, look at brands like New Looxs and Linus. These are satchel and messenger bag styles, often with a cuff to cover the hooks when you are off the bike, and with space for your laptop. Other types are more shopper in style and may not close so securely but are great for a grocery shop or a trip to the farmers' market.

Vintage Velo

I once bought a lovely old pannier in a vintage shop. Although the attachments were broken, I loved it so much I fixed it to my rack with bungee straps. It was not the most practical choice, so when I finally came across the Bobbin Straw Pannier, which resembled my vintage find, I was over the moon. It's very spacious, and its box shape ensures it keeps the contents safe and secure. The practical, modern twist is that it's actually made of woven PVC, so it's water resistant, and has three plastic hooks on the back that clip on to the rack. It zips to close and has an additional flap that goes over the top to keep raindrops at bay. Pannier perfection.

PROFILE
Rachel Bonney, London, bicycle
accessory designer, founder
of Michaux Club
Website: michauxclub.com

What bike do you ride?
A vintage road bike, custom powder-coated
to match my favourite shoes and with
Michaux decal and head badge, and Michaux
handlebar tape.

What do you love about cycling?
Riding my bike is my favourite part of any
day. I love the freedom it creates and the
connection to the world you get from
riding through the elements, seeing seasons
change and engaging with your body and
its surroundings in a way that can be easily
bypassed living and working in a city.

Where do you cycle?
Ironically, since setting up Michaux my daily
commute doesn't involve leaving my house,
so any excuse to cycle is welcome. As much
as I enjoy a relaxing day cycling in the
countryside with friends, I also find heading
into Soho, weaving amongst the traffic, an
invigorating experience.

How did you come to set up Michaux?
Sick of abandoning style for safety on my
daily bicycle commute, and with a love of
tinkering and too much time on my hands,
I made myself a handbag which I could
wear comfortably, stayed waterproof, was
safety conscious and looked smart in work
meetings and out socializing. After several
prototypes, assembled on my kitchen table,
my idea and designs gradually evolved into
the products and brand.

LIGHTS

Brands: Knog, CatEye, Exposure Lights, Bookman.

When cycling between sunset and sunrise, it is an international legal requirement to have both a front and rear light on your bicycle. The front light must have a white beam and the back light a red beam. This is a vital safety measure to ensure you can both see and be seen clearly by all other road users.

Attaching lights

Both lights must be attached centrally on the bike. A common place for the front light is on the handlebars, so you want to position it as close to the handlebar stem as possible. The rear light is usually attached to the seat post. The bulbs in bike lights are usually halogen or LED. It's a good idea to check with the brand that they meet the legal requirement for your country before you buy because legislation may differ from country to country. A simple LED light will come with a mounting bracket that straps around the handlebars or seat post and the light will slot into it. However, there are an ever-increasing number of bike lights on the market in all sorts of shapes and sizes.

When to switch them on

While we mainly think about using lights for night cycling, the law states 'sunset to sunrise'.

So don't wait until it is dark; as soon as the sun starts to go down beneath the horizon, even though you may still be able to see clearly, your lights must go on. And, for all those early risers, if the sun has not popped up and it is still decidedly dusky, light up before you set off.

Things to watch out for

- If you have luggage or a child seat on the back of your bike, a rear light on the seat post may be obstructed. You need to look for a place where the beam will be clear. A good idea is to attach it to the end of the rear rack. You can get a specific rack light if regular rear lights do not fit properly.

- If you have a long coat or skirt that hangs over the saddle it may obstruct your rear light. Try to sit on your coat/skirt or opt for a rack light.

- Flashing lights are now legal in the UK but they must flash between 60 and 240 times per minute. In some countries, however, a flashing light can be seen as an emergency signal, so check with the local laws before you flash ... your lights, that is.

- Additional lights are permitted but they must conform to white at the front and red at the back.

- Keep a spare pair of lights or spare batteries in a safe pocket in your pannier or even rechargeable lights to ensure you don't get caught out in the dark.

• Do not dazzle. There are some bicycle
lights on the market that are excessively
bright – these are often designed for
mountain biking in very dark conditions
and are not suitable for commuter cycling.
Don't assume that the brighter the lights,
the safer you are; in fact, a very bright
light can cause distraction and discomfort
to other cyclists and drivers and could
do much more harm than good. Look
for lights around the 20 lumens mark for
regular commuter cycling.

Bright sparks: Knog

Australian company Knog has
injected some fun into its LED
bicycle lights. The lights are made
from silicone so there's no need
to mount brackets – you simply
wrap them around the handlebars
or seat post in one swift move
and then remove them when you
get off the bike. While the bulbs
conform to the standard colours
of red and white, the silicone
body comes in every colour of the
rainbow so you can have some
fun coordinating them with your
bike, shoes or your mood. But
these lights are more than just
a pretty face, the technology is
there too – in addition to the usual
battery-powered lights, they also
sell rechargeable lights that you
can charge up on your laptop
with a USB and they have several
flashing functions so you can ride
with your own mini disco.

REFLECTORS

A bike reflector is made up of hundreds of cells that bounce the light back to the source when it is shone at them. All bikes made today come with a red reflector at the back, as it's a legal requirement. All pedals will also have an amber reflector on each side. Many bikes will have an additional white reflector on the front and white reflective rims on the tyres, or white reflectors attached to the spokes. If you have an old bike that has not been fitted with reflectors, they are cheap to buy and easy to fit, and you can get them in star and heart shapes if the regular reflectors don't float your boat.

In addition to the reflectors on your bike, there are a range of reflective products that can be worn on your person, some more attractive than others. I will delve into reflective wear in more detail in *Cycle in style* (p138).

PUMPS

Brands: Topeak, Lezyne, Airace, Bontrager.

Pumps come in all shapes and sizes but in recent years there has been a move towards the floor/track pump for ease of use and effective pumping. Handheld pumps that can be mounted on the bike or mini-pumps that can fit in your handbag are handy to have when you are out, but they can be fiddly and you don't always know if you've pumped the tyres to the correct pressure.

A floor/track pump has a sturdy base that supports it on the floor; you unwind the hose and connect it to the wheel's valve. They work with both Presta valves (often found on road bikes) and Schrader valves (usually found on hybrids, utility and mountain bikes), so you don't have the frustration of the pump not fitting different bikes. The pump then remains on the floor and you simply pump up and down. You can then view the pressure gauge on the base of the pump to check you are pumping your tyres to the correct PSI – this term refers to the air pressure and stands for pounds per square inch. (See 'How to pump up your tyres' in *Maintain your bike*, p74)

If you don't want a track pump taking up space in your home, try to find a local bike shop that has a pumping station. Many do have them, including Evans Cycles in the UK, which has a track pump available for use in every store. If you get friendly with your local bike shop and are a good customer, they may even pump them up for you.

WATER BOTTLES

Brands: Sigg, Camelbak, Bontrager, Elite.

While you won't need a full bottle for a two-mile commute, it can be a good idea, especially in hot weather or for longer rides, to have a water bottle on your bike. You will need a mounting bracket that attaches to your frame and a bottle that fits into it. Most bottles are made of plastic and are squeezable with a valve that allows you just to grab it and drink as you cycle. Stainless-steel bottles are also popular as they are durable, so they're more environmentally friendly and can keep drinks cooler for longer.

WATERPROOFS

Most of us have some sort of waterproof jacket that can be worn when cycling; otherwise you can go for a cycle-specific jacket, which will be light and breathable and may be tailored for easy movement on the bike.

For no-nonsense coverage of your bottom half, you could go for waterproof trousers, but these can be awkward to get on when wearing a skirt.

For more information on stylish solutions to those inevitable showers, see *Cycle in style*, p138.

GLOVES

Brands: Knog, AnaNichoola, Sealskinz, BikeTouch Pro.

When cycling in cold weather, the main prerequisite for gloves is that they are WARM. If it's chilly outside, your hands really feel it on the bike. They are completely exposed and will meet cold winds head on. If your hands get cold and start to go numb, or you're constantly trying to pull your

jumper over them, at best you'll have an uncomfortable ride, and at worst an accident. Along with warmth, you also need ease of movement to handle your brakes and react to the road. Skiing gloves or sheepskin mittens are warm, but they may be restrictive. Try leather gloves for casual cycling or, if you are riding further in very chilly conditions, you should look for some cycle-specific winter gloves. Brands such as Sealskinz specialize in gloves that are thermal, breathable and highly waterproof, while allowing freedom of movement – and they have palm padding to boot.

If you are just starting out and need to check maps on your smartphone as you ride, you may want to get a pair of smart gloves. These are full-fingered gloves that have a special fabric on the first two fingertips that allows you to operate a touch-screen phone.

For speedier cycling in warmer climes, you may want to go for padded fingerless gloves. The pads will be placed just at the point where your hands press on the handlebars, so they will help with comfort and grip. They usually have a breathable fabric on the back of the hand to ensure air circulates and to prevent sweat building up. Another good reason to wear gloves is to protect your hands if you fall – damaging the skin on your palms can be very painful and debilitating.

'Nothing compares to the simple pleasure of a bike ride.'
John F. Kennedy, former US President

How to . . .
Maintain your bike

Learning how your bike works can be more interesting and rewarding than you might think, but don't worry, I'm not talking about spending all weekend in the garage, wielding spanners. A general overview of the different parts of a bike and what they do will enable you to look after your bike well, identify problems and even fix minor issues, making you a happier and more independent cyclist.

I was quite simply useless with maintenance when I first started cycling. I knew how to ride my bike and I had a vague idea of how to use the gears but not much more beyond that. I was once inspired by reading an interview with Michelle Pfeiffer where she coolly stated, 'I relax by taking my bike apart and putting it back together again.' I had visions of myself in a checked shirt and dungarees – a tomboy heroine from a 1980s movie – casually tinkering, Pfeiffer style . . .

But the reality was . . . getting hacked off, out in the cold, doing a simple puncture repair, losing my dust cap and my temper, and sulking off down to the bike shop, declaring I quite simply did not have the time to do it myself. Then I bought a second-hand bike and the repair bills started to outweigh what I'd spent on it in the first place, so I embarked on a one-day bike maintenance course. To

my surprise, I found it fascinating to learn how my beloved bicycle – that so cleverly ferried me around all day – fitted together and functioned. Now, don't get me wrong, I still have no intention of spending all Sunday up to my elbows in inner tubes and bike lube (sorry Michelle). But I can now say that I know how my bicycle works and I know what (most of) the parts do.

If, like me, dense instruction manuals aren't really your thing, then this chapter should help. I have received expert help from several wonderful women, brimming with technical bike knowledge. With their help, I shall take you on a non-baffling guide of your bicycle's inner workings, avoiding any confusing bike jargon. This chapter won't be a comprehensive maintenance manual, but it will give you an overview of the basics – and could save you hundreds on bike repair bills!

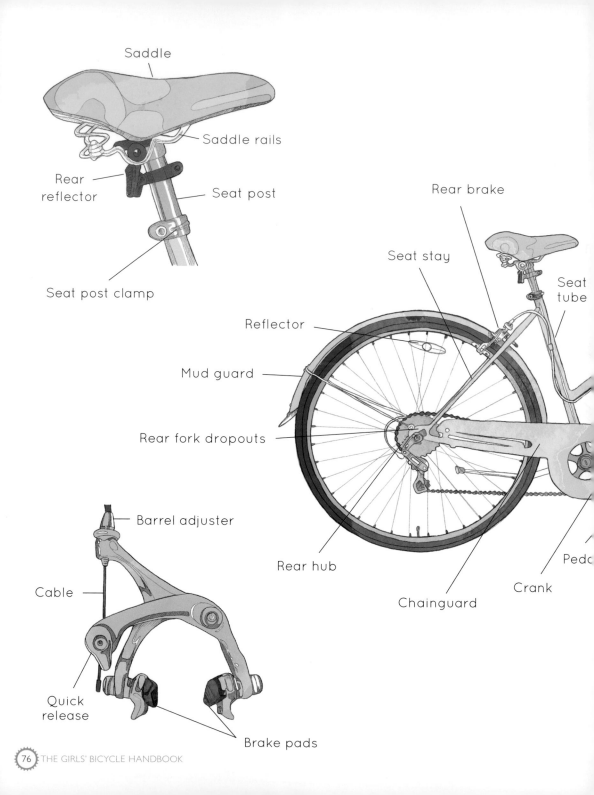

Saddle

Saddle rails

Rear reflector

Seat post

Seat post clamp

Rear brake

Seat stay

Seat tube

Reflector

Mud guard

Rear fork dropouts

Barrel adjuster

Cable

Rear hub

Chainguard

Crank

Pedo

Quick release

Brake pads

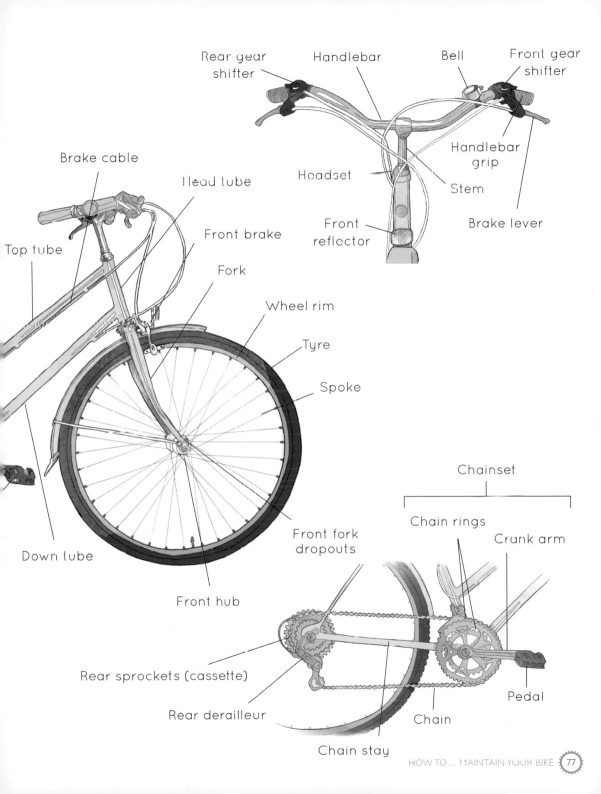

Rear gear shifter

Handlebar

Bell

Front gear shifter

Brake cable

Head tube

Handlebar grip

Headset

Stem

Top tube

Front brake

Front reflector

Brake lever

Fork

Wheel rim

Tyre

Spoke

Down tube

Front fork dropouts

Chainset

Chain rings

Crank arm

Front hub

Rear sprockets (cassette)

Rear derailleur

Pedal

Chain

Chain stay

WHAT'S WHAT ON YOUR BICYCLE

The first step is to familiarize yourself with the various parts of your bike:

Wheels

At the centre of each wheel is a **hub** – the word hub is often used to mean a central meeting point, starting point or hive of activity, and the same goes for the hub of a wheel. Inside the **hub shell** is an **axle** and **bearings** that allow the wheel to turn. The wheel axles fit into the dropouts in the fork (at the front) and the frame (at the rear). If you have an old bike, it's likely to be secured with wheel nuts but most modern bike wheels are secured with a quick-release skewer.

The **spokes** start at the hub and radiate out to the **wheel rim**. The spokes transfer your weight to the rim and ensure the wheel is strong enough to support you. Most bikes have 28, 30 or 36 spokes. The spokes must be tensioned evenly to keep the wheel true (straight). A bent or lose spoke makes for a wonky wheel.

The tyre then goes around the rim of the wheel and the **inner tube** sits inside the tyre – the inner tube being the part that is inflated and the tyre the tougher outer part. The rim is concave to hold the tyre in place. Depending on the size of tyre, it can take some elbow grease to lever the tyre on and off.

Brakes

The most common type of brake is a **rim brake**, which is so called because it slows the bike down by putting pressure on the rim of the wheel. The **brake levers** on your handlebars are connected to **brake cables** that then connect to the **brake arms** and **brake pads**, which sit on the wheel. When you pull on your brake levers, the cables tighten to cause the arms and pads to clamp on to the rim and stop the wheel turning.

There are three types of rim brake: **calliper**, **cantilever** and **V brakes**.

The other type of brake that you might find on a bike is called a hub or disc brake, which slows the wheel down by putting pressure on the hub.

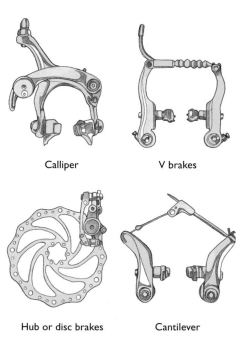

Calliper

V brakes

Hub or disc brakes

Cantilever

Handlebars and steering

Your **handlebars** connect to your **handlebar stem**, which connects to your **head tube**, which joins up to your **fork**. The fork then attaches to the front wheel hub. You also have a set of components called a **headset** and a **steerer tube** that fit inside the head tube. The fork slots into this and swivels around on ball bearings, allowing the handlebars to turn from side to side. This clever series of connections allows you to steer your bicycle.

There are two types of headset: **threaded** and **threadless** / Aheadset.

Threadless

The way to tell if you have a threaded or threadless headset is to see if your handlebar stem has a clamp at the side. If does have a clamp, it is threadless and needs spacers inserted to adjust the length. If it does not have a clamp but just has a hole at the top for an Allen key, it is threaded and, by loosening it at the top, you can move the handlebar stem up and down.

A good way to remember it is to think of threaded headsets as having a stem that is threaded through the frame.

Threaded

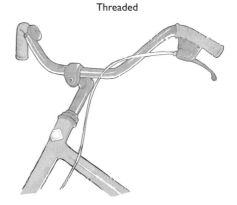

Frame

The frame is the core of the bike on to which all the other bits attach. The centre consists of the **top tube**, the **seat tube** and the **down tube**. Towards the back you have the **chain stays** and the **seat stays**, both of which connect to the rear wheel. At the front, the **head tube** connects to the **fork**, which connects to the front wheel. Women's frames traditionally have a slanted top tube, the original purpose being for ladies to straddle the bike easily when wearing a dress or a skirt. Although it seems like an old-fashioned notion, I am all for a slanted top tube as it makes mounting and dismounting easier, whether you are wearing a skirt or trousers – you can bring your leg across at the front of the bike rather than swinging it over at the back.

The drivetrain

The drivetrain system converts the power produced by your pedalling into movement of the back wheel, thus propelling you and your bicycle into motion. This is called the 'transmission'.

As you pedal, the motion passes through the **crank arm** and moves the **chain ring** round. The chain sits on the chain ring and travels around to the rear cog (**sprocket**). Depending on your gearing, you will either have a single sprocket or multiple sprockets (called a **cassette**) and that starts to move too. The sprockets are attached to the rear wheel axle, causing that to turn and move the rear wheel around.

Gears

The gears on the bike help you navigate different types of terrain. You choose your gear by feel: if you are going up a hill and it's hard to pedal, get into a lower gear. If your legs are spinning and you're not going fast enough, get into a higher gear.

Gears are part of the drivetrain and determine your speed. On some bikes, like a BMX or a single-speed bike, there may only be one, but most bikes have multiple sprockets. On a multiple-geared bike there are two types of gear: **derailleur** and **hub**.

Derailleur gears: Most modern bikes will be fitted with a **derailleur** gear system (see right). The name originates from the French word meaning to 'derail a train',

because, when you change gear, the chain is simply lifted (derailed) from one cog and put on another.

The derailleur is the mechanism that moves the chain up and down the cogs and is sometimes called the 'mech'. It is operated by a cable, which is connected to a lever (or gear shifter), positioned on the handlebars.

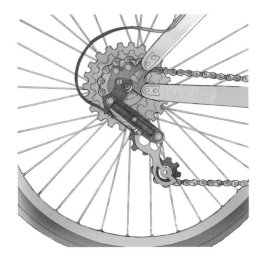

Many bikes have a front and rear derailleur, meaning that you can move not only between multiple cogs on the rear wheel but also between chainrings on the **chainset**, where the cranks and pedals are attached. To calculate the total number of gears your bike has you need to multiply the number of sprockets on the rear cassette by the number of chainrings on the front chainset.

The smallest sprocket on the cassette at the back is the highest gear (harder to pedal, for going fast); the biggest sprocket is the lowest gear (easy to pedal, for going up hills).

Confusingly, the chainrings on the chainset work in the opposite way: the biggest ring is the highest gear (hardest to pedal) and the smallest the lowest (easiest). So, if you have a huge hill to climb, you would get into the gear using the biggest cog on the back and the smallest ring on the front.

You have gear shifters for both front and rear derailleur on the handlebars. The right shifter is for the rear gears and the left is for the front gears. The idea with derailleur gears is that you have lots of options and subtlety between the feel of the gears. You have to find the perfect combination for the terrain by experimenting – riding around and shifting between them. You need to be pedalling for the gear to change. Expect some clunking with derailleur gears but they should click into place with one full rotation of the pedals.

Types of bike that have derailleur gears include mountain bikes, road bikes and hybrids.

Hub/internal gears: With three-speed hub gears, it really is as simple as one, two, three. It's a very clever gear system invented in 1902 by bike-obsessed teacher Henry Sturmey and bike mechanic James Archer. It was then developed by Raleigh and became the standard gearing system on the majority of British-made bikes. I won't go into the technical details of how these gears work because a) it is ridiculously complicated, proving a challenge for many bike mechanics, and b) they are almost impossible to break. The gear mechanism is sealed inside the hub

of the rear wheel – the illustration below shows what it looks like within the hub. You can't see it, it rarely needs maintenance and doesn't get dirty or need lubrication. The only thing that may need adjusting is the cable attached to the gear shifter. This needs to be at the correct tension to pull through the gears. If it's not, the gears will slip or delay.

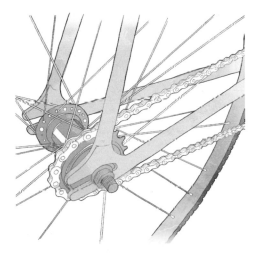

You will find the traditional three-gear hub system on European utility bikes, vintage bikes and traditional-style town bikes. There are also now more modern hub gears that go up to eight gears from brands such as Shimano and SRAM.

You don't need to get in a greasy mess trying to put your chain back on and you can change gear whether cycling or stationary. It is the ideal stress-free gear system.

Saddle

The saddle is of course for accommodating your bottom. On the underside, it has **saddle rails**, which attach it, via a **saddle clamp**, to the **seat post**, which connects to the frame.

Saddles come in all shapes and sizes, which can cause confusion when trying to find the most comfortable ride. When you cycle, your weight should be supported by your seat bones (the bones at the very bottom of your bottom). If you are leaning forward on your bike and still putting pressure on the saddle, you could find that the weight is transferred to your much more sensitive 'lady's area'. This, in short, can hurt like hell – both when cycling and for days after.

Here are a few tips for getting the right saddle for you and your derrière:

Wider saddles: Women generally have a wider pelvis than men and therefore have more shapely bottoms, so a saddle that is slightly wider at the back could be more comfortable. Wider saddles work well on bikes with a more upright riding position, where your weight falls naturally on the seat bones. If your saddle is too narrow in this relaxed, upright position, your seat bones will hang over the edge, putting pressure on the wrong bits.

Saddles with holes: If you cycle in a more dynamic, forward-leaning position and cycle for longer periods of time, it may be inevitable that your lady parts feel the brunt of your saddle. A good option here is to try a saddle with a kindly placed hole in the middle to prevent pressure. Some women do find that the edges of the hole can chaff, however, so this may not be a solution for all. But I would advise taking a look at the brand

Specialized for this type of saddle. They have done loads of testing to produce a range of saddles specifically for women. Check out their saddle-finder on their website (see p220).

Leather saddles: The advantage of a leather saddle is that, over time, it gives and moulds to the shape of your bottom, so in a month or so you have your very own tailor-made saddle. Leather is also breathable, so it prevents you getting hot and sweaty down there, and many leather saddles are sprung so they soften the blow when cycling over lumps and bumps. The added perk is that classic leather saddles look fabulous. I would recommend a Brooks saddle – I had a B67 Brooks saddle for several years, which I was very happy with. Sadly, it got stolen, highlighting the downside of having such a desirable saddle – best to get a small lock to attach it securely to the rest of the bike (see p51).

Three saddle no-nos

Don't blame your saddle if you've not been on your bike for a while

This scenario is common with people who do longer rides but tend to have a break over the winter months. You get back on your saddle, set off for an ambitious ride in spring and return home with a sore bottom, convinced a new saddle is the answer. The problem is more likely to be that you are not yet as fit as you were and therefore have been pushing less with your legs and putting more weight on your bum. So the answer is to build up slowly and get your fitness level back, rather than waste cash on a new saddle.

Don't be fooled by a very soft, cushioned saddle

Although a saddle that feels as comfy as an armchair when you first sit down might be tempting, over time this is not a great option. Your seat bones will sink into a very soft saddle, causing the pressure to transfer to your sensitive area, and the softness could also cause chaffing.

Don't tilt your saddle too far forward

It may seem like the perfect solution ('long bit at the front hurts, so push long bit out of the way') but, while a very slight tilt may relieve some pressure, if your saddle slopes down too far, YOU will slope down too. This will cause you to put too much pressure on the handlebars, which will lead to arm, shoulder and neck pain.

COMMON NOISES AND WHAT THEY MEAN

Often the first sign of a problem with a bike is a noise. Bicycles are quiet beasts, so when they start making noises it's a sign that something is up. If you hear a noise, focus your attention on where it's coming from and use the following guide to pinpoint the problem.

Brakes squeaking or grinding

If there is a squeaking/squealing noise or a lower pitched grinding noise when you apply the brakes, it could be one of the following:

• The brake pads are worn and need replacing.
• The brake pads are not hitting the wheel rim in the right place and need realigning.
• You have an old bike with steel rims. This means a certain amount of squeaking is unavoidable. You can try replacing the pads, but if this does not work, look on the bright side – at least everyone knows when you're arriving.
• You have oil or grease on the rims or pads. The best thing to do is give your rims a scrub with steel wool or very fine sandpaper and file the brake pads to roughen the surface.

A regular noise every wheel rotation

If you hear the same consistent noise each time the wheels go round, it could be one of the following:

• The wheel is not installed straight – try reinstalling it. If the noise persists, the wheel could be bent and you will need a bike mechanic's help.
• The brake pads are rubbing and need realigning.
• The mudguards are loose and rubbing on the wheel; they need tightening.
• A clicking sound could be the spokes rubbing. Try oiling the intersections (where two spokes cross).

Pedals clunking or clicking

If you hear clunking or clicking noises coming from your pedals:

• First, check the pedals are tightened snugly on the crank arm; if not, tighten.
• Then, check that the crank arm or pedal isn't hitting something on the way round, possibly a kickstand, or pump mounted on the frame.
• If the noise persists, it could be a problem with the bottom bracket, so it might be best to get it checked out by a mechanic.

Chain area squeaking, clicking or skipping

If you hear squeaky noises or skipping sounds coming from the chain area:

- First, clean the chain and apply lube,
- If you are still getting a gentle twittering sound, it could be the gear pulleys/pivots that need oil. See 'How to clean and lubricate your bike', p99.
- If lube has not worked and the chain is skipping as you cycle, it could be either the gears that need indexing, a stiff link, a worn chain or a worn cassette. It is probably best to get a mechanic to check it out and replace any worn parts.

Rattling or jangling

If your bike rattles and jangles when you go over bumps, it may be a loose accessory:

- Check all racks, baskets, child seats, lights and bells are securely attached.

Quick check: A B C D

This is the easiest basic check. Do it once a week as a quick way to make sure everything is in working order. It need not take more than five minutes.

Air: Squeeze tyres at the side, on the tyre walls (not on the top of the tyre); if they give, pump them up.

Brakes: Push bike forwards and backwards, and test both brakes.

Chain: Run through all your gears; check for rust and add a few drops of chain lubricant, if necessary.

Direction: Stand in front of your bike, clamp the front wheel with your knees and try to twist the handlebars from side to side. The handlebars should not move when your knees are holding the front wheel securely. If they do move, you need to tighten the headset. See the M check on the next page.

THE M CHECK

A good way to check all the moving parts of your bike is with an M check, so called because the order in which you check the different parts of the bike forms the letter M.

The M check is thorough and is only needed if you have not ridden your bike for some time or if you've bought a second-hand bike; BUT it's a great way to give yourself an overview of the various parts of the bicycle and alert yourself to what can go wrong. Wedge the book open at this page, get your bike in front of you and go through the M check from start to finish. Or, just dip in and out when a problem, irksome noise or your curiosity draws you to a certain area.

Start at the front wheel

- Crouch next to the wheel, hold it with both hands and give it a wiggle to check it is securely attached at the axle. If there is any movement you will need to tighten the wheel nuts or quick release.

- Lift up the handlebars so the front wheel comes off the ground and spin the wheel round to check it moves freely. A wheel that doesn't move freely could be bent or the brake pads could be out of place.

- Strum the spokes as if you were playing a harp to check that none have come loose or have snapped off.

- Give the wheel a squeeze on the tyre wall to check it is pumped up enough. Inspect your tyre wall for splits and cracks, and check the tread of the tyre is not completely worn down. If one tyre needs replacing, the chances are the other one will too, so it's best to get them replaced at the same time.

Move up to the brakes

- Push the bike forward to check the right-hand brake and backward to check the left-hand brake.

- Check the brake cables for rusting or corrosion; they run from the lever to the brake arm, down on the wheel.

- Check if the brake pads are worn, these are the parts of the brake that come into contact with the wheel. They usually have a wear line to show when they need replacing.

- Check that both brake pads hit the rim at the same time; if they don't, you may need the brakes realigning.

Now check the handlebars

- Check the handlebar stem is tight and secure; stand in front of the bike with your hands on the handlebars and hold the front wheel between your knees. First, check the handlebars are aligned with the wheel. Then try to turn the handlebars while still clamping the wheel. They should not move. If they do, tighten at the top of the stem with an Allen key.

Check the pedals and crank arm

- Pull and push the crank arm (the arm connected to the pedals) to check it is securely attached to the bike.

- Spin the pedals and then make sure there is little or no movement when pulling or pushing them away from the crank arm.

Check the gears and chain

- Check for grit and dirt: such matter can stick to the oil on the bike chain and can cause a grinding effect. If the chain is looking grubby, give it a clean and apply lube (see 'How to clean and lubricate your bike' on p99).

- Check for chain wear, sagging or rusting. If it's looking the worse for wear, the chain may need replacing.

Then move up to the saddle

- Try to wiggle it to check it doesn't move. If it does, check the quick release is secure, or tighten the nut on older bikes.

And, finally, down to the rear wheel

- Repeat the wheel-and-tyre check from the front wheel on the rear wheel.

And your M check is complete!

'HOW TO' GUIDES

HOW TO PUMP UP YOUR TYRES

Keeping your tyres pumped up to the correct pressure will prevent punctures and make cycling more pleasurable. If the sidewalls (rather than the top) of your tyres are squidgy or you are below the lower limit of the PSI range for your tyres, it's time to get pumping.

1. Invest in a floor/track pump; they may be slightly more expensive than a hand pump but the time and effort it saves you will soon make up for it. See the 'Pumps' section in *Accessorize your ride* (p71).

2. Check the PSI range for your tyres. PSI stands for pounds (of air) per square inch and basically means the air pressure. All bike tyres are different, and manufacturers indicate the specific PSI range for each tyre on the sidewall. Road bikes will have a higher pressure, on average between 90 and 120 PSI, while mountain bikes and hybrids are usually lower, between 50 and 90 PSI. You want to have the pressure in your tyres around the middle of your PSI range.

3. Unscrew the dust cap and identify if you have a **Schrader** or **Presta** valve. The Schrader valve (mountain bikes, hybrids and traditional bikes) is short and wide and all the same width, while the Presta valve (road bikes) is long and thin, with a pointy end and a little circular screw nut at the top.

a) If you have a Schrader valve, it is a simple case of pushing the valve into the right hole on your pump.

b) If you have a Presta valve, make sure you loosen the little brass nut first, and then attach the pump. Be careful not to snap off the nut when pumping.

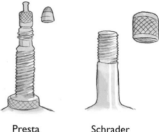

Presta   Schrader

4. The beauty of a track pump is that it will have a hole for each valve: identify which hole fits, push the valve in the hole and tighten the lever. Most modern hand pumps have levers too, so similarly push the valve in and pull up the lever.

5. Start pumping. With a track pump, you can see the dial go up; if you are using a hand pump, you will need to stop and check with your fingers to see when the sidewalls of the tyre are hard.

6. Once you have reached the required PSI (or hard sidewalls) you can stop pumping. Release the lever. Some air will escape at this point but don't worry – it's not escaping from your tyre; it's just the air left in the top of the pump.

7. If you have a Presta valve, screw up the little brass nut. Replace the dust cap and you are ready to go!

HOW TO PUT YOUR CHAIN BACK ON

If you have derailleur gears, a fairly common problem is for the chain to come off the chainring. It's a quick and easy job to pop it back on.

1. Lean your bike against a solid object, with the wheel touching, to prevent it moving around. If your bike has a kickstand, that will work too.

2. Get a stick or tyre lever ready to use so that your hands won't get too dirty.

3. Place your finger on the tab at the back of the rear derailleur and push it forward to give your chain more slack.

4. Then, using your stick or tyre lever, pull the chain up and place it on the smallest chainring at the front. Doublecheck the chain is sitting correctly on the chainring and that the teeth of the ring are connected and sitting in the right place along the chain.

5. Then let the rear derailleur go back into place and the chain will tighten.

6. Check it's on correctly by lifting the bike up and moving the pedals backwards. Then cycle the bike slowly to be extra sure.

HOW TO ADJUST YOUR SADDLE

Saddles are made to be adjustable to ensure that you get the right riding position depending on your leg length and preference. (See 'What size do I need?' in *Find a bike you like*, p42.) Many modern bikes will have a quick-release mechanism so adjusting the saddle is easy, but older bikes will have a bolt and nut that needs loosening with an Allen key. Once loosened or released, you will be able to shimmy the seat post up or down to make the saddle higher or lower. Then, make sure it is straight and tighten it up again.

You can also adjust the position of the saddle in relation to the handlebars – closer or further away – by sliding it along on the rails underneath: just slightly undo the nuts under the saddle and wiggle it backwards or forwards.

HOW TO ADJUST THE HEIGHT OF YOUR HANDLEBARS

Threaded headset

Unscrew the bolt at the top of the handlebar stem with a 6 millimetre Allen key. Pull the stem up if you need your handlebars to be higher or push it down to lower them. Make sure that you do not pull the handlebars up over the height restriction line, as the stem could fall out when riding. Ensure the handlebars are straight and then tighten the bolt back up again with the Allen key.

Threadless headset

The height of the handlebars on a threadless headset (or Aheadset) cannot be adjusted quite so easily. First, you need to unscrew the headset bolt and step clamp bolt with Allen keys. You can then remove the handlebar stem and use spacers to adjust the size but you will usually only be able to adjust it by a few centimetres. It is very important when investing in a bike with a threadless headset that the handlebars are in a good position for you before you buy.

HOW TO REMOVE WHEELS

You may need to remove a wheel to fix a puncture, travel with your bike or ward off thieves. If it's your first attempt, it may be easier to do it with the bike upside down but you can do it with the bike upright.

Removing the wheel

1. If removing the rear wheel, you need the chain to be on the smallest sprocket, so adjust the gears to the highest setting before you start. (If you have hub gears, this does not apply but you will need to disconnect the gear cable before you start. If you are unsure how to do this, check with the manufacturer or ask a bike shop.)

2. Release the brake cables. With some bikes you can release the cable by squeezing the brakes together by hand and pulling the cable gently out of its resting place. Other bikes may have a quick release on the brake lever but, if you are not sure, it's best to check with your specific brand and type of brakes. One way to release the wheel without disconnecting the brakes is to deflate the tyre slightly so the wheel can clear the gap between the brakes.

3. Push out the quick-release lever while simultaneously unscrewing the nut at the other side until you can pull the wheel free.

Old-school bikes: If you don't have a quick-release lever, you will have a bolt and nut instead, which requires a 15 millimetre spanner to undo.

4. When the wheel is loose, you should be able to ease it out and remove it from the bike. With the rear wheel, ensure you unloop the chain from the sprocket as you remove.

Installing the front wheel

1. With the bike upside down, push the wheel back on to the frame, ensuring the axle fits into the grooves on the fork (the dropouts) and that the wheel is centred between the forks.

2. Then tighten the quick release by turning the nut and then the lever and, when it feels stiff, pushing the lever down. Or, for older bikes, tighten the wheel nuts with that 15 millimetre spanner.

3. If you disconnected the brakes, reconnect and you are all done.

Installing the rear wheel

1. When putting the rear wheel back, ensure the cassette on the wheel is on the right-hand side of the bike (when the bike is upright).

2. You need to align the chain with the small sprocket, as it was when you removed it.

3. Drop the wheel in, checking the axle is sitting on the grooves on the frame (the dropouts), and then turn the pedals to ensure the chain is connected.

4. Then tighten the quick release, as with the front wheel, by turning the nut and then the lever. When it feels stiff, push the lever down. For older bikes, tighten the wheel nuts with a 15 millimetre spanner.

5. Reconnect brakes, if you disconnected, and you're all done.

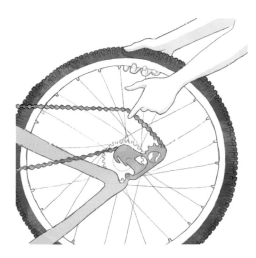

HOW TO MEND PUNCTURES

Do you have painful memories of puncture repairs from the past ... scrabbling around with inner tubes in buckets of water and almost having a hernia trying to get the tyres off and on again?

There's no doubt about it, if you've not done one for a while, puncture repairs can be a touch awkward. But a little practice and you'll be puncture-repair perfect. Give yourself time, get the correct equipment and follow this step-by-step guide.

The perfect puncture repair

You will need: Tyre levers (metal are better than plastic), a Biro (most repair kits come with a crayon but a Biro is much better for marking the puncture accurately and clearly), a small square of sandpaper, a tube of rubber solution, rubber patches, chalk and a serrated edge to grate the chalk.

Step 1: Remove the wheel from the bike. (See 'How to remove wheels' on p93.) Then deflate the inner tube, which will make it much easier to get the tyre off. For Schrader-valve tyres, remove the dust cap and push the end of a matchstick or pen nib into the valve – the air will then shoot out. For a Presta valve, when the brass nut is loosened, you should be able to press on the valve with your finger and air will escape.

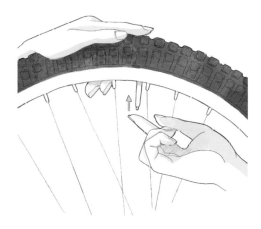

Step 2: Insert one tyre lever under the beading of the tyre and pop it off the rim. The levers have a hook on the other end, as they are designed to hook on to the spokes to keep the tyre dislodged from the rim – so put the first one in position. You can then put another lever under the beading and gradually work it all the way round the tyre, releasing the circumference of the tyre on one side only.

Step 3: Now get your fingers in under the tyre and pull the inner tube out – ease it out all the way round and gently pull the inner tube valve out of the wheel rim. Take extra care when removing the valve, as a damaged valve is not repairable.

Step 4: Once the inner tube is out, you can remove the tyre from the wheel completely. Check the inside of the tyre for glass or debris, turn the tyre inside out to get a good look or run your fingers along the inside (but be sure to wear protective gloves). Then, check the metal rim of the

wheel and again remove any sharp bits that could cause further punctures. If you find anything poking through the tyre, like a nail, remove it.

Step 5: Find the pesky hole. A bucket of water is not usually necessary unless the hole is very small. Instead, inflate the inner tube with your pump, hold it close to your ear and turn it round gradually, listening for the sound of air escaping. When you hear it, bring the inner tube a few centimetres from your lips – your lips are very sensitive, so you should be able to feel the air escaping, and also see the hole that close up. You should use a well-lit room or do this outdoors.

Step 6: Grab your biro and mark the spot with a large X so you can be sure you will be putting the patch on centrally. Then, run the sandpaper lightly all over the area around the hole to help the rubber solution adhere to the inner tube.

Step 7: Apply the rubber solution and be fairly generous so there aren't any gaps once the patch goes on. You then need to wait until the rubber solution goes tacky: you can tell it's ready when it looks more matte and less shiny – the warmer it is, the quicker it will be. When it is ready, stick your rubber patch on and press it down, holding it for 30 seconds or so. Make sure all the edges are sealed.

Step 8: Grate the chalk against the serrated edge or the sandpaper over the rubber patch. This neutralizes the excess rubber solution to stop the inner tube sticking to the tyre. You will then need to leave it another 20 minutes or so to ensure it has dried fully.

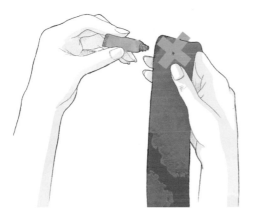

Step 9: Finally, take the paper or plastic off the back of the patch, blow up your inner tube (before it goes back in the tyre) and check that there is no air escaping anymore – to confirm your repair has worked and make sure there isn't a second, smaller puncture.

Step 10: When you are confident it's fixed, deflate the inner tube about halfway to make it easier to get back on. Put one side of the tyre back on to the wheel. Insert the valve of the inner tube through the hole in the wheel rim and then ease the inner tube inside the tyre all the way around. Then, put the other side of the tyre on to the wheel rim. Lastly, pinch the tyre together and look all the way round the edge to make sure that the inner tube has not got caught anywhere. Pump up and put the wheel back on the bike (see p94).

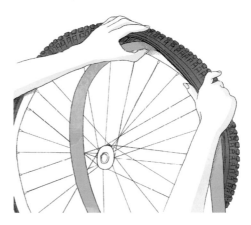

Q: My tyres are really stiff to get back on; what can I do?
Try to be patient – it may take a little while, especially if your bike is new.

Start by hand, pushing the loose side into the rim and working your way around the tyre, until you reach the point where it feels tight – there is usually about 10 centimetres of tyre that you can't push in. Get one of your tyre levers and push it between the tyre and the rim to lever the tyre in. Then, when there is only a small section left, use the palm of your hand and role the tyre in, pressing hard to ease the last bit over the edge.

If you are still struggling, don't be ashamed to take your wheel to a bike shop and ask them to walk you through it. Most mechanics are happy to show you some tricks, and many bike shops run free maintenance classes. There really are little subtle ways of doing this that make it much easier, and they're hard to know unless you do it all the time.

THE LAZY CYCLIST
Puncture repair the lazy way

• Carry a spare inner tube with you – inserting a new one is much easier than fixing one.

• Get it repaired at a bike shop. There's no shame in getting a puncture repaired by a professional, especially if you are short of time and need to be back on the bike asap. Just be sure to hunt around for a good price for the job, so the hole in your tube doesn't make too much of a hole in your wallet.

• Prevent the puncture in the first place, by keeping your tyres well pumped up and checking them for any glass or splinters after a ride.

HOW TO CLEAN AND LUBRICATE YOUR BIKE

Cleaning and lubricating (which just means oiling) your bike does not have to be a laborious task performed before and after every ride – unless you're into that kind of thing, of course. Here are a few pointers so you know what needs doing and when.

Clean the wheels

Run a damp sponge along the wheel rim to get rid of dirt and build-up that may prevent the brakes from working efficiently. Then also run the sponge along the tyre itself, checking for glass or any other sharp bits that could cause a puncture. There are no strict rules about how often you should clean your wheels. Common sense should prevail – a slightly grubby wheel is nothing to be worried about but one caked in mud or street grime would probably welcome a scrub.

Clean and lube the drivetrain

Clean: It's important to clean all the old lube off before you apply the new. Cleaning the chain with degreaser or washing-up liquid should do the trick. Use a dishwashing brush or a toothbrush to give it a scrub and get in all the nooks and crannies.

Lube: Use a bottle of chain lube. Put newspaper down first to catch the drips, then dribble the oil along the chain. Also dribble lube into the pivots of the derailleur gear mechanisms. If you are not sure where

the pivots are, change gear while stationary and you will see them move. Some bike oils come in a bottle with a thin pointy applicator to get the lube in the right place.

Q: How often should I clean and lube my chain?

This entirely depends on how much you cycle, what type of cycling you do and in what weather conditions. If you commute regularly, it's probably best do it roughly once a month, but if you only pootle around town, once every couple of months will do. If the chain is making noises, this is a sign it may need cleaning and oiling.

A FINAL WORD

If you are a complete newcomer to bicycle maintenance, don't expect to master it overnight. It will take time to build up your knowledge and acquire the practical skills. It can be tremendously satisfying to fix even the most minor issues. I have been known to leap into a smug celebratory dance after accomplishing the simplest of maintenance tasks! And even being able to take your bike into a shop for a repair and explain what you think the problem is (rather than just mumbling that something's wrong and committing to a full service because you don't have the bike vocab to say otherwise) can be a big bonus for both your ego and your wallet.

PROFILE
Megan Somerville, from Toronto, Canada, lives in London, Re-use Coordinator at Bikeworks

What bike do you ride and why do you like it?
I am all about worry-free cycling, that's why I ride a single speed. I can go at my own speed and I don't feel like I'm part of the rat race.

What basic maintenance advice would you give to someone who's just started cycling?
I would advise that you know a few basics so you can either make easy fixes yourself or walk into a bike shop and be specific about the problem. A basic maintenance course is worth its weight in gold — it will give you all the basics you need to know and will help you diagnose what might be wrong with your bike.

Know how to fix a puncture but always keep a spare inner tube on you. In fact, if you go to the shop to buy a spare, buy three, then you will always have a extra one when you need it. I wouldn't advise fixing a puncture by the side of the road — you want to be doing it in front of the TV as it can take a bit of time to do it properly. But if you carry a spare inner tube in your bag, you can just change it and bring the old one back home to repair. Keep the new tube in an old sock so it doesn't get nicked on something in your bag. You can also use the sock to check for pieces of glass in your tyre (the cotton will catch on it) and you can wipe your hands

on it when you are done. Another good tip is to **invest in tough Kevlar tyres** (a very strong synthetic fibre) that will prevent you getting too many punctures in the first place.

Keep your chain clean and properly lubricated (one drop in each link and then wipe off the excess). I use rubbing alcohol to clean my chain, because it evaporates; you can also use surgical spirit or even — at a pinch — nail polish remover.

Listen to your bike and be able to detect when there is something wrong. Does it sound the same? Does it feel the same? Brakes feel stiff? Oil the cables. Bike feels sluggish? More than likely your tyres need pumping up. It's about being able to feel when there is a problem and addressing it before it gets worse.

Another great tip is to **write down all the details of your bike** on a card and keep it in your wallet: tyre size (which is written on the side of your tyre), inner tube type, whether it's a Schrader or Presta valve, and brake pad type. Then, when you get to a bike shop, you know what you are looking for.

What equipment would you recommend getting?

Track pump, puncture repair kit, spare inner tubes and an Allen key set.

What other advice would you give to women when it comes to urban cycling?

One main problem is that women are not taking their space on the road – cycling too close to the kerb can be very dangerous, as you have no escape route. Another big no-no is sitting alongside a lorry – they cannot see you and you are putting your life into their hands, not your own. Lorries are the number one killer of cyclists. Just hang back and wait. Allow some time in your journey for delays, then you can just chill out. I would suggest an urban cycling course to anyone who is riding in a city – no matter how long you have been riding your bike for. You need to be constantly aware of traffic and just generally learn how to manage the flow of vehicles instead of trying to duck and dive.

What I find interesting about cycling is that throughout history it has been so much about freedom and independence for women and, even if we don't register it consciously, it's still there. My friend back in Canada called me recently – she is moving abroad and she said, 'Help! they've boxed up my bike – what do I do?' The bike is her freedom and she feels lost without it.

'Toleration is the greatest gift of the mind; it requires the same effort of the brain that it takes to balance oneself on a bicycle.'
Helen Keller, American deaf and blind political activist, 1880–1968

5

How to . . .
Keep your bike secure

One of the few perils of being a cyclist is bicycle theft. In the US, four per cent of all crime is bicycle related and, in the UK, someone's two-wheeled friend is stolen every minute. Unfortunately, recovery rates are not great – around five per cent – so you want to do all you can to protect your beloved bicycle and save yourself the upset and disruption of having it stolen.

If you stop, you must lock

No matter what kind of bike you have or what type of cycling you do, if you intend to leave the house and stop anywhere for any length of time, you will need to lock your bike up. I have heard countless stories of people who leave their bike for 'just a second' to grab something from their house or pop into a shop. And in that second the bike is stolen. So, much as the idea of propping a bike up against a wall and waltzing off without a care in the world appeals, it's just not possible if you want to hang on to your bike.

LOCKS AND LOCKING

The first and most important step is to get yourself a good-quality lock. See 'Lock it up' in *Accessorize your ride*, p50.

If you want to be extra vigilant, get yourself another lock and double-lock it! Two locks of different types will require the thief to have two tools to break both, so the job is already much harder for them. For example, you could use a D lock around the back wheel and through the frame and a chain lock through the front wheel and front of the frame – but don't forget to lock both to the bike stand. Alternatively, if carrying two heavy locks is too much of a strain, try a D lock and an extension cable. Lock the frame and one of the wheels to the bike stand with the D lock and then wrap the extension cables through the D lock and through the front wheel, so the front wheel is locked on to the rest of the bike. This is a particularly good locking method if you have quick-release wheels.

Tips on how to lock it up

Leave as little space as possible between the lock and the bike

If you are just using one D lock, try to secure one of the wheels and the frame so the lock is snug and more of the bike is secured. This may not always be possible, depending on what you are locking your bike to, and may be another reason to keep extension cables on you as a back-up.

Point the lock with the keyhole facing downwards

One thieving tactic is to pour liquid in the hole so that you can't unlock it, giving the thief more time to work on breaking the lock.

Make your bike unrideable

Take the saddle or front wheel off, especially if you have quick-release wheels, to deter thieves and prevent them riding away on it as if it's their own.

Check it before you leave it

Be sure to give your bike and lock a quick once over before you leave – you wouldn't be the first person to lock the frame to itself but not actually secure it to the bike stand or vice versa.

Tips on where to lock it up

Use bike parking

Wherever possible, try to find specific bike parking. Many pro-cycling governments are aware that safe cycle parking is an essential facility if they want to promote a healthy cycling culture. If you live in a city where bike riding is growing, you may find that more parking is popping up or being incorporated into new developments. But we are not all this lucky and you may have to make do with what the street can offer.

Lock it to the most secure thing you can

Lock your bike to the most secure, most immovable object that you can find. Avoid short posts, as the bike can be lifted over them. Even signposts that look secure can have their signs unscrewed so the bike can be pushed over the top. Avoid wooden fences, drainpipes or objects that could easily be sawn or broken to release the bike.

Choose busy areas

When parking your bike on the street, go for a busy area with lots of activity, as opposed to quieter roads or alleyways. It will be harder for thieves to steal your bike if there are lots of people around.

Don't abandon it

Although you are fully entitled to stay out all night, don't leave your poor little bike on the streets to fend for itself. This gives the thief plenty of time to work on your bike in darkness with no one around.

Don't park your bike in the same public place each day

This gives thieves a chance to assess your lock and know which hours you leave it there so they can come along fully prepared to steal it.

Innovative Bike Parking

British company Cyclehoop designed the **Car Bike Port**, which aims to promote and encourage cycling in towns and cities worldwide and has been installed in the UK, Sweden, New Zealand, Australia, Germany, Finland and North America. Its eye-catching, car-shaped design houses ten parking spaces for bikes but fits into one car-parking space, conveying the message that bicycles are more space-efficient than cars. The Car Bike Port even has an in-built pump station so not only can you park your bike and make a point, but you can keep your wheels spinning all the smoother when you leave.

the train station, and houses an impressive 970 bikes.

The **bike rack** pictured below is part of a unique architectural project in Superkilen, a public park in Nørrebro, Denmark. The area is ethnically diverse and the idea was to create an urban landscape that celebrates this multiculturalism with materials and structures from all over the globe. The variety of objects in this park represent, and have been chosen by, the 60 different nationalities in the surrounding area. This curly and colourful stand would certainly brighten up my bike-parking experience.

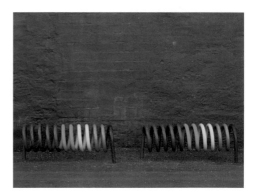

The **Bike Apple** is a huge bike garage, shaped, as you might have guessed, like an apple. It is situated in the Dutch town of Alphen aan den Rijn, right next to

Park next to a better bike

I'm not quite sure how this affects your bicycle karma, but a sneaky trick is to park your bike next to a more expensive set of wheels. Your bike will pale into insignificance when the thief is faced with the flashier model.

Finally, if you can't stop worrying about your bike . . .

Ride a less attractive, less expensive bike

Thieves with half a brain are going to go for bikes that will make them money. Although inexpensive bikes do get stolen, to a professional bike thief, an old bike that carries little value is a far less attractive option.

Get a second bike

If you are worried about leaving your dream bike out and about, you could get yourself a second, cheaper bike that you use when it needs to be left for some time. I have my very favourite bike that I keep indoors at night, and a second bike — an old Raleigh Caprice, picked up on eBay — that I use for the school run and the shopping, and she lives outside (under a cover). While I would be gutted if she got stolen, I would have a more easy-come, easy-go attitude than I would with my more expensive set of wheels.

SECURITY AT HOME

Although it may be less likely for your bike to be stolen from outside your house than from the street, as bicycle thieves get sneakier, it's becoming more and more common. The main concern when thinking about storing your bike at home is how to keep your bike safe, but you also need to think about keeping it dry and easy to access, if you are cycling regularly. It's all very well locking it away in the shed at the bottom of the garden but, if you are cycling to work every day, you may want it in a handier position to save those precious minutes in the morning.

INDOORS

Try, where possible, to get your bike indoors. If you don't have enough space, see if any of the following solutions might help you squeeze it in:

- Go for a small/lightweight model of bike, or at best a folding bike, so it can easily be carried upstairs or tucked away discreetly in a hallway or corner.
- If your sofa is against a wall, try bringing it forward a foot and sliding your bike behind it.
- There are a range of stylish racks and shelves that can be mounted on the wall to take your bike off the floor and prevent it clogging up the hallway. If you like the way your bike looks, you can take it one step further and display it centre-stage in your living room, as an interior design statement, for all to see.

Stylish wall hangings for beautiful bicycles

Fixa bike shelf from Chrome is mounted on to your wall, your bike slots into the groove and you have extra space for your helmet and lights or a vase of flowers on top.

The Trophy bike holder from Outline Works Ltd is shaped like a bull's head and will keep your trusty steed off the floor, holding it firmly in place with its horns. The elegant, streamlined design is made from solid steel, with a soft-touch coating that won't damage the bike. It will also accommodate a bike with a slanted top tube, as long as the slant isn't too extreme.

OUTDOORS

If, try as you might, it's just not practical to get your bike inside or a 'no bikes in the house' law has been laid down by others, here are a few tips for outside storage:

Don't lock it to a rickety fence
or anything else that can easily be broken.

Look at getting a bike stand installed
These range from wall anchors that can be bolted to the wall, accommodating a lock, or a bike stand that can be bolted or cemented into the ground.

Tuck your bike away
Try and put it in a corner where it's out of sight and cover it with a nylon or PVC bike cover (often called bike pyjamas). Not only will this make the bike less visible to thieves but it will also keep it dry in wet weather and prevent rusting, damage to the brakes, and that all-too-annoying damp bottom that comes with a wet saddle.

Bring your bike inside
If you're going on holiday or even if you are just away for the weekend, bring your bike inside before you leave. My bike was stolen when I was away for a weekend; they must have been watching the house and knew no one was about.

Sheds can be a good place to keep your bike dry and out of sight but they can also be easy to break into. You may need another method of locking the bike securely, inside the shed.

Bike bunkers are tough little units made of galvanized steel, making them much more secure than sheds. Designed specifically for bikes, they are compact and so can fit in small outside spaces. They also provide extra security, with internal locking features or mounting points where locks can be attached.

Thoughts for the front garden

Plantlock from Front Yard Company is classed as an immovable object, weighing more than 75 kilograms when planted up, and you can lock two bikes to the handles securely. It can also really brighten up a dead bit of space at the front or back of a building and allow you to indulge in a spot of gardening.

Show your bike some tough love with this heart-shaped Princess Kate bike stand available from Bike Dock Solutions. It can be bolted or cemented into the ground and you can secure two bikes to it by both the frame and front wheel.

Make sure you're smiling instead of those pesky bike thieves by installing a Smile bike wall anchor from H-B Designs on the wall of your house. The smile is big enough to get a sturdy D lock through and you can choose from a range of smiley colours to match your bike or your front door. Remember, you'll need to use security screws for this, but they also have a helpline if you get stuck when installing it.

'She who succeeds in gaining the mastery of the bicycle will gain the mastery of life.'
Frances E. Willard, *Wheel Within a Wheel: How I learned to Ride the Bicycle*, 1895

WHAT TO DO IF YOUR BIKE GETS STOLEN

You need to take action straight away by filing a police report. There are then various things you can do to try and get your bike back. Your chances of being reunited are not high, I'm afraid, but it is certainly possible. Stories often circulate about people wrestling thieves and successfully reclaiming their bike but this is not advisable. Take a look at the tips below for action you can take yourself but always be sure to get the police on the case when it comes to confrontation, instead of wading in yourself.

File a police report
Call the police and give them as much information on your bike as possible: brand, colour, frame number and any other distinguishing features.

Set up alerts on both eBay and Gumtree
You can customize and save specific searches with descriptions of your bike that a thief might use to sell it.

Spread the word online
Use Facebook, Twitter and bike forums, posting a picture of your bike and asking people to keep an eye out for it.

Ask in local bike shops
It is always worth asking around local bike shops, especially those that deal with second-hand bikes, to see if anyone has tried to sell them your bike.

Miki Yamanouchi, London, UK

When my bike got stolen, I refused to sit by and just let the thief get away with it. After reporting it to the police, I went on to Gumtree and eBay and created an advert offering a reward if anyone could get my beloved bike back to me. I also bluffed slightly, saying it was an extremely rare, one-of-a-kind model. I then laminated a dozen reward posters with an image of my bike and plastered them all over the area from which it was stolen. Two weeks later, I got a call from the police; my bike had been found abandoned in an old lady's garden. I cried – tears of happiness, of course. The thief had tried to scratch off the brand name and head badge but had not succeeded so had dumped it. My bicycle and I had won. Hurrah!

ADDED PROTECTION

Bike tagging
This is a way to register your bike so, if it does get stolen and then retrieved by police, it can be traced back to you easily. It involves your bike being marked with a unique code that corresponds with your bike frame number and personal details. In the UK you can get your bike tagged directly by the police. They hold sessions on a regular basis throughout London or you can register online and buy tamperproof stickers to place on the frame. The stickers also act as a deterrent to thieves who will not want a tagged bike on their hands.

Insurance
There are two ways to go with insurance: you can either get your bike covered with your home contents plan or you can get specific bike insurance. Some home contents policies may stipulate that your bike must be kept indoors for it to be covered, so double-check the fine print.

A good policy will insure you for more than just the replacement of your stolen bike: it may also provide third-party and personal injury cover, in case you are in an accident, overseas cover for holidays, and cycle rescue if you end up stranded with a broken bicycle. All this can cost about the same as a D lock for a year's cover. It doesn't mean that you can get lazy with your locking, though; most cycle insurers will demand that your bike is locked with an accredited lock to an immovable object at all times when unattended.

The six stages of bicycle grief

Having had my precious Pashley Poppy stolen from outside my house recently, I know first-hand the pain and upset that ensues. I have spoken to many other women (and men) who have found themselves in the same unfortunate position, and I know I am not alone in feeling pretty heartbroken. The emotional connection you have with your bike can be extremely strong. So don't feel silly if your emotions get the better of you; the important thing, however, is to take some action and do your very best not to let it happen again.

Stage 1: Pure shock
You don't quite believe it and you try to come up with a rational explanation as to where your bike has gone, rather than accepting the ugly truth. 'Maybe my neighbours have moved it, maybe a friend has borrowed it or maybe aliens landed and fancied a bike ride ...' etc, etc.

Stage 2: Anger and emotional outbursts
When you stop kidding yourself and realize it has been stolen, you feel ANGRY and then more ANGRY and, if you're an emotional sort, like me, you may shed a tear or two.

Stage 3: Take action
Report it to the police. Get the word out

there to family, friends and your local bike community. I didn't find my bike but I did get a lot of advice and very sweet condolences, as well as offers of bike loans from friends, which were very much welcome.

Stage 4: Your life becomes a logistical nightmare
Before you can get a replacement bike, you realize all your routines and carefully planned schedules are scuppered. It takes half an hour longer to get everywhere. You find yourself doing a lot of rushed walking while muttering obscenities about the lowlife that nicked your bike.

Stage 5: Get over it and get a new bike
At some point, you have to wipe away those tears and start to plan your replacement bike.

This is where kind offers of bike loans should be gratefully accepted to prevent Stage 4 from reoccurring. I had not insured my bike (silly me) so had to assess my finances to see what I could afford. The thought of getting a new bike can lift your spirits and be an exciting opportunity to try a new type of bike.

Stage 6: Ensure it doesn't happen again
I have to admit that I did not do everything I could to ensure my bike was safe but, once you have a bike stolen, it does make you wise up to bike security. I took several steps with my new set of wheels, including buying a better lock, bike tagging and even investing in a smaller bike that would fit snugly in my hallway. Fingers crossed, my new bicycle and I will not be parted for some time.

PROFILE
Emilee Tombs, Cardiff, Wales
Blog: bikebelles.wordpress.com

What bike do you ride and why
do you like it?
I ride a vintage Raleigh Caprice, bought for
me by my boyfriend from a charity shop
for my 21st birthday. It's white with yellow
flowers adorning the frame. About a year
after I got it, it was stolen from outside a
shop near my house, despite having a lock
on. I loved it so much that I tracked down an
identical one on eBay and re-bought it. It's
beautiful and practical. Her name is Fleur.

What city do you cycle in and what's
the cycle scene/community like?
I ride mostly in Cardiff, where I'm studying
for a master's at the moment. My ride into
uni is one of the nicest I've ever ridden, and

it's pretty convenient – the road from my
house snakes down through the park and
runs parallel with the river; in the spring, the
park is full of wild garlic and cherry blossoms
and it makes me happy to have my bike.

I started a blog for bike lovers when I started
my course and I found the community in
Cardiff very receptive. Turns out a lot of
people here love their bikes as much as I do!
I have even found a place called the One
Mile Baker – they deliver bread and cakes
within a one-mile radius and all deliveries are
done by bike.

How are the roads in your city –
good for cycling?
The roads in Cardiff are the downside.
Although many of them do have cycle lanes,
they've been very poorly maintained and are
peppered with potholes, which has caused
me plenty of problems since I've been here.

How does cycling benefit your life?
I couldn't live without my bike now! I use
it to do my shopping (I stash veg in the
front basket), to get to uni (it only takes 10
minutes, whereas it's a 30-minute walk) and
it allows me to get almost anywhere in the
city – Cardiff's quite small. I love it!

What's your favourite outfit to
cycle in?
My favourite outfit to wear would be my
long grey marl dress with a leather jacket and
of course my bright purple bucket helmet
(safety first!). I like to ride in skirts like the
French girls do!

6

How to . . .
Cycle safely

If you feel apprehensive about cycling in traffic, you are certainly not alone. One of the biggest factors putting people off cycling is a fear of the dangers of the road. The advice here comes from my own experience. I am not a qualified instructor, and always advise getting professional training, but hopefully the things I've learnt along the way will be some help. With practise and determination you'll pedal past the panic and will be amazed at how quickly your skills grow.

I have never learned to drive and, as a child, my urban cycling was limited to gentle laps around a very quiet cul-de-sac. But, with a professional cycling lesson, and plenty of practice and observation, I was amazed at how quickly my skills developed and my confidence grew. It takes determination and an openness to learn, but when you finally pedal past the panic and feel confident cycling in traffic, it is enormously empowering.

BEFORE YOU BEGIN

Back in the saddle

If you haven't ridden for some time, don't launch yourself on to the high street during rush hour without any practice. The expression 'it's like riding a bike', meaning you never forget, may be true but if you're having problems recalling the last time you rode a bike, some off-road practice is a very wise move.

Don't be embarrassed if you're a little bit wobbly to start off with, especially if you have a new bike; it may take some time to get used to it. Walk your bike to a park or open space (try to find smooth tarmac surfaces rather than grass or rough terrain) and practise. Embrace your inner 11-year-old and have some fun playing around: go fast, go slow, bum on saddle, bum off saddle, use the brakes, the gears, and turn corners – no skids or wheelies, though, please.

Once you feel confident on your bike, you can try more structured exercises to prepare yourself for the roads. But first, check your cycling position is fit for urban riding.

- Check you can touch the floor with tiptoes while sitting on the saddle, to ensure you can stop securely.
- Check you can reach the handlebars with ease, so you can cycle with your hands over the brakes.

Have some training

I'd highly recommend a bike lesson or training if you're at all nervous or confused about urban cycling. It doesn't have to be a long, drawn-out process — a one-off professional training session or some guidance from an experienced friend can work wonders. Being scared and unsure of what you are doing is not a recipe for calm, confident cycling. Speaking as someone who came to urban cycling with bundles of enthusiasm but no experience, I can honestly say the two-hour lesson I had was invaluable. Cycle training for adults is often free or heavily subsidized; in the UK, go to cycletraining.co.uk for more details.

Cycling for the non-driver

Many cyclists don't drive, riding a bike being their main mode of transport. And hurrah for all the eco-tastic, self-propelled people out there. But busy road systems to a non-driver can be a discombobulating nightmare so you need to get in the know. You can't cycle in a bubble — it will all too soon get popped.

- Start to take more of an interest in the way traffic functions and flows — road etiquette, junctions, lane discipline — and focus and observe what's going on from the passenger seat, or from your seat on the bus.
- Ask family and friends about a certain junction or situations that confuse you to try and get your head around how they work.
- Study the Highway Code. You should try to learn this as if you were learning to drive. It may be a laborious task, but it will make you a safer cyclist on the roads.
- And lastly, of course, have a lesson, have a lesson, have a lesson.

ESSENTIAL SKILLS

Here are a series of exercises to help you master the essential skills needed for cycling safely. Start by trying the exercises off-road, and then, when you are confident, apply them to the streets.

Stopping and starting

Urban cycling involves a lot of stopping and starting. You'll need to be able to stop confidently and steadily at traffic lights, give-way lines and roundabouts, and be ready to start again as swiftly and as smoothly as possible. Here are a few tips for successful stopping and starting:

Change gear: If you're cycling in a high gear, change down to a lower gear well before you stop. This will allow you to get going quicker when starting up again. When shifting gear with derailleur gears, it will take one revolution of the pedals for the chain to shift on to the correct cog and for the gear to change – so allow plenty of time to change down through the gears. If you change while you are stationary, you'll have a clunky adjustment as you push off again and the chain might fall off!

Pedal position: As you're coming to a stop, try to position your pedals so the pedal you're going to push off with is raised and ready to go. Move your pedals backwards as you're braking. You can then rest easy with one foot on the ground and one foot on the pedal. You can adjust your pedals once stationary (by pulling the pedal backwards with your toes), but if, for example, the lights change the second you stop, this action will delay you getting going again, so it's a good habit to get it in place before stopping.

Exercise: To practise stopping and starting, set yourself a point in the distance to stop at. Ensure you change down through the gears and that you get your pedals in the right position, and come to a stop with one foot on the ground and one on your push-off pedal. Hold the position and then start cycling again. Getting this right and avoiding wobbly starts will be a huge help to you once you face the streets.

Emergency stop

You never know when you might have to make an emergency stop: a pedestrian may step into the road, apparently from nowhere, or traffic ahead may halt abruptly. You need to be prepared to bring your bike to a standstill quickly and safely. Focus on pushing your body weight back and down on to the saddle while braking, and lock both arms before securing your feet on the ground. This will prevent you flipping over the handlebars due to the force of the brakes.

Exercise: Cycle at a reasonable speed and give yourself a certain point to stop, or ask a friend to call out to you. As soon as your friend calls, make the emergency stop and be careful not to put your feet on the ground too early! Once you are stationary, keep your hands on the brakes to secure the bike until you are ready to get going again.

Signalling and turning

Clear arm-signalling is essential when cycling in traffic. When turning left or right, you will first need to look behind you and then hold one arm out, while retaining balance. There is a lot going on. There is a left turn I make frequently, on a downhill slope after a roundabout, so I need to be extra vigilant when looking behind me and need to be able to signal left while braking with my right hand. Balance and control are vital. Here are a few exercises to prepare you:

The high five: Take a friend to the park to be your high-five partner. Ask them to stand about 20 to 30 metres away and raise their hand. Cycle towards them and give them a high five. This exercise will get you used to taking one hand off the handlebar while in motion. A fun one to do with kids!

DO look back: Checking traffic behind you is a crucial part of cycling on the roads and it is of the utmost importance when making a turn. Sometimes you just need a quick glance but other times you may need to sustain the position for a few seconds to make eye contact with the driver behind and make sure that they have seen you and clocked that you're about to manoeuvre. To perfect this skill, practise twisting round and looking behind you while cycling in a straight line, first keeping both hands on the handlebars, and, when you feel confident, taking one hand off and twisting round a little further. Try this at varying speeds and hold the position for one, then two, then three seconds. You may feel shaky to start with, but

keep going until you can look back and keep your balance. You could also get a friend to stand behind you and ask you how many fingers she's holding up – so you have to turn and focus!

Look back and signal: You now need to combine both of these skills for a complete signalling and turning sequence. Give yourself a certain point to turn, cycle towards it, looking behind for two to three seconds while retaining your balance, and then make a nice, clear arm signal for two seconds. Have a quick look behind, just before you turn, then make the turn.

Safe swerving

Unfortunately, most road surfaces have various lumps, bumps, potholes or clusters of glass that are safer swerved around than cycled over. You need to be able to make a quick, balanced swerving movement without losing control or getting in the way of traffic. The key is to keep your body facing forward and only make a minor steering adjustment with your arms, so it's a quick, controlled movement and doesn't affect the rest of your body or send you off-course. Try to avoid sudden, wide swerves, especially when you have traffic around you, as it will confuse drivers and could put you in danger.

Exercise: Establish an obstacle ahead or lay a hat on the ground, cycle towards it, swerve to avoid and resume your position cycling forwards. Remember to focus on making it a concise movement that doesn't take your direction off course.

POSITIONING: SEE AND BE SEEN

One metre in

The most common mistake a beginner cyclist makes is to cycle too close to the kerb, the logic being that this will keep her out of the way of the traffic. In fact, the opposite is true. Despite what some people think, cars do not want to hit cyclists. It involves far too much messy paperwork. The majority of accidents happen when the motorist has not seen the cyclist. If you tuck yourself into the edge of the road, you are often out of the line of sight of the driver and can easily be missed. Instead, you need to take an assertive position that makes you as visible as possible, about one metre from the edge of the road or the parked cars.

Despite having read about this rule, it wasn't until I had a more experienced cyclist observe me during my cycling training that I realized I would tend to start in this position but gradually creep further and further into the kerb. It was almost as if, as a cyclist, I was apologizing for being on the road. There were two things going on here: firstly, I had read the rule but didn't really understand the reason behind it; and secondly, I didn't believe that I was entitled to take that position in traffic. By cycling behind my instructor and watching her retain this position for some distance, it finally sunk in that I had every right to do it too. It wasn't going to upset anyone and it wasn't going to put me in danger.

So, instead of hiding yourself from the traffic by cowering at the kerb, make sure you cycle in the correct position, about one metre from the edge of the road or the parked cars, and no closer than half a metre.

- This position makes you more visible to traffic behind you as well as traffic pulling out from side roads.
- This position will prevent you getting hit by the door of a parked car – a very common cause of cycle accidents.
- This position will ensure you are visible and that you have a clear view of the road, especially if there are parked cars along the side of the road. Maintain this position and do not duck into the spaces between parked cars, as you will have a limited view of the road and may be invisible to traffic at times.

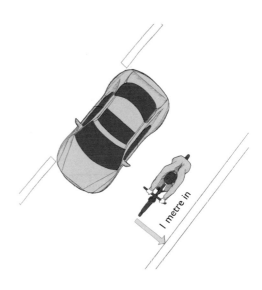

1 metre in

The more space you give yourself, the more space other road users will give you. If you give yourself ten centimetres, the car driver thinks that's all you need and will only allow you that when passing you. But if you give yourself one metre, the driver is inclined to give you more space.

Cycle Zen: While maintaining a visible position is very important, you must also apply some common sense and be considerate to other road users. When Diana Ross sang 'It's a game of give and take', she may have been talking about love, but the same goes for sharing roads. If there's a lot of traffic building up behind you, pulling in to let them past might be a decent thing to do and will take the pressure off you. In the same way, if it's wiser to stop and let oncoming traffic past, instead of pushing your way through a tight gap, do it – your safety and cycle karma will be much improved. Let's have some love and peace out there on the roads.

Exercise: Find a residential street with cars parked either side of it; ask a fellow cyclist to cycle behind you to keep an eye on your positioning. Also, concentrate on negotiating with cars as they come past, giving way when you can but without compromising your safety.

Primary/central position

There are certain situations when you need to position yourself in the middle of the lane (as if you were a car) – this is called the primary position.

The primary position may feel scary to start with and it does take some getting used to, and even some courage on the odd occasion when you get comments from drivers about hogging space! But you must remember that you do have the right to do it. If you are in doubt, and you don't feel comfortable, get off the bike rather than muddling through, but in the following situations assuming the central position in a confident manner is strongly advised:

When approaching a junction where traffic is building up, don't try to weave your way in and out of traffic or hover on the far left or right – this is when you want to be as visible as possible to traffic behind, so they can see you and see your signal. Take the primary position and wait until the traffic moves. Having a car in front of you and behind you may seem daunting at first but it's safer than having a row of cars to your side, unaware of your presence. Assuming the primary position will also mean that cars cannot turn across your path.

When starting the manoeuvre of a right turn or when approaching a roundabout, getting yourself central in the lane prevents traffic unsafely overtaking you and puts you in the most visible position.

When the road narrows or has cars parked along it, or any similar situation where it would be unsafe for cars to overtake you.

Turning left

When turning left, you need to look behind in plenty of time and signal clearly. If there are vehicles behind and you feel you need to be more visible, don't be afraid to move into the primary position, providing it is safe to do so. It may seem counter-intuitive to take this central position when you are turning left, but again it is about being visible to the traffic behind (who may also be turning left into your path), and it will also ensure you have a good view of the road you are turning into. You should also glance over your left shoulder to check for other cyclists who may be coming up behind you on your left. And when the coast is clear, make the turn.

Turning right

Turning right is trickier and can feel more stressful than turning left, as you have to cross both lanes of traffic to get to where you want to be. But for your own safety and peace of mind, you must prepare for the right turn in plenty of time and be in full view at all times. These three steps should help you get that right turn right.

1. Give yourself plenty of time: Start to prepare by looking behind you and signalling approximately 25 to 30 metres before the turn, (you may need to signal earlier if traffic is moving fast). Find a gap in the traffic, signal right and move into the primary position. Don't leave it until you are almost upon the turn; this will make it very hard to get into the right position and could annoy or confuse traffic behind.

2. Get into the right position: If you can't make the turn straightaway due to oncoming traffic, wait in the primary position, parallel to the central line of the road you are turning into, and hold your signal. Depending on the width of the road, traffic may be able to pass you on the left, but if it's not safe, they should wait.

3. Don't worry about traffic having to wait: Wait until there is a safe gap and then move promptly. You might feel a little exposed to start with, but this will usually only be for a matter of seconds and it is safer to wait than to take a risk.

Don't be too concerned if you find right-hand turns hard to start off with, especially on busy roads. And don't be afraid to pull in safely and cross by foot rather than rushing it and feeling unsure. Check out the situation from the pavement and figure out where you need to start preparing and where you need to stop to wait for oncoming traffic to pass — so you know for next time.

Overtaking traffic

As a cyclist, you will often have to pass vehicles, whether they are parked or have temporarily stopped at the side of the road – buses and taxis are prime examples – or are waiting to pull out or turn in. Keep an eye on the indicator lights of the cars in front of you, as well as looking for any wheels facing outwards in a line of parked cars – it's a sign they're about to move out in front of you and you could be in their blind spot.

When overtaking is required, it is vitally important to check for traffic behind and to indicate clearly that you will be moving out into the road to pass the vehicle. If there are several stopped vehicles, it may be best to take the primary position (i.e. in the middle of the lane) to avoid having to weave in and out of traffic and to ensure you remain visible.

In the middle of a traffic jam, traffic may be stationary in multiple lanes, but we cyclists are free to move and overtake. However we still have to be careful. Pedestrians may attempt to cross the street through the static traffic and step out from behind cars suddenly, without warning. Scooters and other cyclists, less careful than us, may also be weaving their way through heedlessly – so take care. In many cases, especially where you can't see clearly to your endpoint (such as overtaking a long bus or lorry), it is much safer to wait in line with the traffic.

Changing lanes

Roads often divide into two lanes as they approach junctions. Try to identify as soon as possible which lane you need to be in, depending on which way you want to go, so you're not trying to squeeze your way across traffic at the last minute. Generally speaking, the left lane is for traffic turning left and going straight on, and the right lane is for traffic turning right. Sounds simple, but you need to check the arrows (which will be clearly marked on the different lanes on the approach to the junction), in order to ensure you can signal and move into the correct lane as early as possible.

When changing lane, always ensure you are as visible as possible to traffic behind you. Sometimes the road will be divided into three lanes and you may be required to cross a middle lane in order to turn right. You need to make sure you signal well in advance in order to let the traffic behind you know of your intention and hold that signal while traversing BOTH lanes. If it's a new road to you and you don't think you have time to get to the far right lane, don't be afraid to pull in safely, observe, and try it again next time when you are familiar with the situation. Likewise, if you find yourself in the wrong lane, it's better to pull over when safe rather than panic and swerve.

Roundabouts

The rules of roundabouts can be puzzling, and tackling them can be a challenge, especially for the non-driver. The purpose of a roundabout is to keep traffic moving and drivers are urged to act swiftly as soon as a gap appears. This can feel stressful for us cyclists, as a) we can't accelerate as fast as cars, and b) we need to trust that the drivers on the left will register us as a road user and stop to give way to us. If you have no experience of the wondrous invention that is the urban roundabout, you might find this little roundabout guide helpful.

- **In a roundabout, all vehicles give way to traffic entering from the right.**
- Before entering the actual roundabout, you need to stop and wait for a space. You have right of way over traffic entering the roundabout at the next entrance (to your left).
- You need to be alert and ready to go when you can, and be assertive when pulling out. It will help if you are in a mid/low gear so you can start up quickly yet still be able to pick up speed.
- Good positioning is vital on a roundabout. The diagram below shows the correct positioning when turning left, going straight on or turning right. Always signal your intentions clearly before you enter a roundabout.
- Indicate left once you have passed the last exit before yours, and look behind you to check the way is clear for you to make your exit.
- Turning left is the easiest manoeuvre on a roundabout as the principles are the same as turning left at a T-junction.
- Don't feel bad about waiting for a space. Sometimes it does take ages and you're being a responsible road user by waiting.
- Be decisive once the way is clear – the worst thing to do on a roundabout is

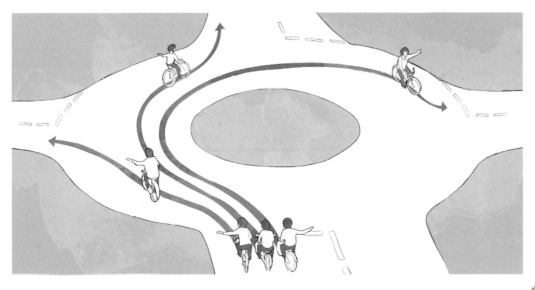

dither as it sends confusing signals to other road users.

• Note, these instructions are for a single-lane roundabout; tackling multi-lane roundabouts can be hectic, so look for cycle-specific crossing points or subways first. Ensure you know what lane you need to be in well in advance, or ask a more experienced cyclist to take you through it first.

ON THE ROADS

Push rather than panic

Don't be afraid to dismount and push – at any time, but especially when you first start cycling. I have already touched on this point but I want to reiterate it, as it was key for me when learning to cycle in a very busy city. If you're approaching a junction but are unsure of what to do, pull in safely and get off your bike. Take a look at the junction from the safety of the pavement, maybe watch other cyclists and try to figure out what your correct move should have been. You can either attempt it again or just cross as a pedestrian and get back on the road at a point where you feel more comfortable. The key is to find the balance between confidence and caution, advancing your skills and trying new things but not feeling pressurized or pushed into situations that scare or confuse you.

There is nothing wrong with hopping on and off your bike as you please, as long as it's done safely (always dismount with your bike between you and the traffic and get on to the pavement, if possible). This goes against the philosophy of some diehards who think you're somehow less of a cyclist if you choose to jump off and push here and there. This is a load of rubbish. There's no shame in being safe.

Find quieter roads and off-road routes

Although the most direct routes can be busy major roads, you will often find there is a much more chilled cycle route on smaller residential streets. It may take a little research, but sniffing them out can be well worth it. My local swimming pool is about two miles away but the direct route is along a very busy road with a monster of a roundabout at the end. After a little experimentation, I found a route that winds through residential streets, through a very attractive business park with a waterfall and ducks, and ends with a cycle-specific crossing point at the roundabout – a perfect stress-free cycle.

When planning a cycle ride, look on the map to see if there are any smaller roads that run in parallel to the main road you need, or see if you can see any parks that you could cut through or rivers and canals with paths alongside. Canals were built as a means of transporting goods and people into the city and can often provide a great car-free route. You will need to keep your speed down and your eyes peeled for pedestrians when cycling along canals or through parks.

Pedestrians

When you are cycling off-road, pedestrians are your traffic. Pedestrians may not be as intimidating as cars but they still need to be passed with care as they are not looking out for you or expecting you – and they always have right of way. If you are coming up to pedestrians ahead who are blocking your way, ring your bell in plenty of time so they have a chance to move to the side. You may need to ring a couple of times, as they could be engaged in conversation, have headphones on or be a rabble of noisy kids (with headphones on!). As you approach, it's a good idea to make it clear which side of the path you are going to pass on. If you just cycle right through the middle, they may be confused which side to go and you will all be doing a merry dance. Don't feel rude for ringing your bell, but don't ring it unless it's necessary and give them a nice smile and a thank you as you pass.

Listening

Being able to hear what is going on around you is an invaluable asset for us cyclists. It gives us an extra sense of awareness of cars and other people on the road. So don't plug your earphones in or wear hoods and hats that hinder your power to hear; your ears are an essential safety tool when out on the bike.

Cycle lanes

Cycle lanes and paths differ greatly from country to country and city to city. In countries such as Holland and Denmark, where the cycling culture is very established and cycling as transportation is mainstream, the cycle lanes are often segregated from the traffic. There is either a physical kerb to separate them or the cycle lane has its own traffic lights, with special care being taken to ensure the bicycle is the quickest route into the city – not the car. Innovative systems like this are a treat for cyclists, but for this reason they can get very busy and you need to stay ultra-aware of other cyclists around you.

In cities where cycling is not yet mainstream but is growing and being encouraged, cycle lanes are improving in quality and quantity. This is a real, positive sign of change to urban infrastructure. However, many cities and towns do not have this luxury, and cycle lanes often feel more like a gesture than a safe route. At worst, a cycle lane can be a sporadic line on a bumpy part of the road that may decrease your visibility. It's important not to follow a cycle lane blindly, presuming it's the safest option. Think about

your positioning and, if you cannot see and be seen, you are entitled to cycle outside it.

Bus/cycle lanes

In Germany, France, the UK and the USA, bus/cycle lanes are becoming more commonplace. As the name suggests, this is a lane reserved for buses and bicycles. When first cycling along these in London, I was sceptical, but it works quite well. It's a leapfrog of sorts – when a bus is stationary, picking customers up, you indicate and carefully overtake. Keep an eye out for the indicator lights on the stationary bus as you prepare to overtake. If it's about to move off, its right-hand indicators will start to flash, so hang back. If you know it's safe to overtake, indicate, and cycle past. The bus driver will be trained to look out for bikes before pulling out so, as long as you don't cycle too close, they will spot you. Both the UK and Germany have reported a decrease in injuries from implementing bus/cycle lanes.

Heavy goods vehicles (HGVs)

Collisions with HGVs (massive lorries) account for over 50 per cent of all cycle injuries and fatalities. But this is not because the drivers of these vehicles are out to get us defenceless little cyclists, it's mainly down to the driver not being able to see the cyclist, due to the size of the vehicle and the blind spots this creates. It is essential that you avoid the following four positions or actions when encountering an HGV on the road:

1. Don't undertake the HGV on the left-hand side. This is where the driver has the biggest blind spot, so if you sneak up closely on the left-hand side and they do not see you and either move off or turn left, you could be hit. Just wait a metre behind the lorry until the traffic starts to move again. Even if the cycle lane takes you down the side of the HGV, DON'T FOLLOW IT!

2. When traffic is stationary, don't weave in and out and come round the front of the lorry. The chances are that, by passing the lorry at the side or by the front of the cab, the driver will not have seen you and could start moving off and hit you.

3. Be cautious when overtaking to the right: the blind spot is not as big as on the left, but there still is one, and the driver may pull off without having spotted you.

4. Don't stop anywhere to the left or right of the lorry – even by the side of the cab, the driver still can't see you; you either want to be behind the lorry or in front of it. A good way to ensure the driver can see you if you are in front is to turn around and get eye contact. If behind, you should always leave a bike and a half, in case the HGV starts to reverse.

Safety in adverse weather conditions

Rain: When it's raining, you need to be extremely alert and take extra care on the roads. The roads can be slippery, so take it slow on corners, keeping as much weight as possible on the outside pedal to ensure you stay balanced. Rain can also reduce the friction between the brake block and the wheel rim, so, if you have rim brakes, they may not work as effectively and you may need to brake sooner and/or harder. Resist the childish urge to plough through puddles – submerged potholes can catch you out. To prevent rain going in your eyes (or on to your glasses) and affecting your vision, try a peaked helmet or hat.

Wind: Cycling against strong winds can give you a real workout and your journey may take longer than usual. Be sure you have no loose clothing, scarves or hats, or anything that could be swept out of a basket or pannier with a gust of wind. If winds are strong enough to send you off balance, don't risk it – leave the bike at home.

Snow: If you are cycling regularly in snowy conditions, you will need a special type of studded tyre to ensure you don't slip on icy surfaces. If you only get a few snowy days a year, a chunky hybrid tyre or mountain bike should suffice. The key is to try to stay relaxed; ensure you brake earlier and don't make any risky moves or take tight corners.

Safety at night

It's essential that you have a red rear light and a white front light attached securely to your bike, and you must check they are working and are not obstructed by any luggage or clothing. You could also opt for some reflective elements about your person (see *Cycle in style*, p138). And although cycling on smaller, quieter roads is great when cycling by day, they may not be as well lit, so a bright main thoroughfare could be safer. When cycling by night, you need to keep an extra eye out for pedestrians, as they don't generally make a habit of attaching lights to themselves or wearing reflective clothing, and around pub-closing time their road-crossing skills leave a lot to be desired. It goes without saying that cycling after a few drinks in the pub yourself is not wise (see *Cycle for fun*, p184).

Learn from others

A great idea is to go out with friends who are more experienced cyclists or to join guided group rides. This can be a real confidence booster and will give you a chance to get out on the roads that you feel too nervous to tackle by yourself. Keep your senses alert and think for yourself while soaking in what the more experienced cyclist is doing. Ensure you don't lapse into a relaxed state and passively follow – you won't learn anything and it could be dangerous.

Going it alone

You only learn how to do something properly when you have done it by yourself. How many times have you been taught something – cooking, DIY, IT – and feel sure you know exactly how to do it but, when you're trying it alone, it's somehow not so easy? Well, the same goes for cycling. Taking lessons and cycling with others is a great way to learn but it's not until you get out on your own that your own skills truly develop and your confidence grows. You need to cycle independently to truly master the skill. And once you do, the sense of achievement is awesome.

Confidence and state of mind

While technical cycling skills are of high importance, having the right state of mind will keep you safe on the road. In an ideal world the traffic around you will behave rationally and courteously, but sadly this isn't always the case, especially in busy traffic. Regular cycle commuters advocate cycling 'defensively'. This means that, as well as signalling clearly and obeying the rules of the road, you need to stay fully aware of the vehicles (and pedestrians) all around you – and actively anticipate what others are about to do or might do. Cycling defensively means that you will automatically avoid situations that put you in danger. So, be decisive on the road, keep your wits about you and, most importantly, enjoy the ride.

PROFILE
Diane Jones Randall, New York, USA

Where do you cycle and why?
I'm a 51-year-old African-American New York who recently rediscovered her childhood bike and even more recently overcame a fear of riding on the streets of Manhattan to become a daily commuting biker. I don't drive. I've always used public transportation in the city, but wanted a means of transport that felt like 'mine'. I hadn't ridden a bike since my childhood 1974 English Raleigh and that had been disassembled and tucked away in a closet for 25 years.

What bike did you start with?
To begin my bike journey, I bought a mountain bike because I thought it would be sturdy in the city. When I started, I was terrified of riding in the Manhattan streets with traffic, so I spent the first weeks gingerly coasting around my apartment complex and illegally on sidewalks close to home. I love the city.

As cute as my mountain bike was, I wasn't comfortable with the forward-leaning position and I had multiple parts replaced to make it more upright. Although my mountain bike had never seen a mountain, I loved the sense of security that allowed me to bounce over potholes with abandon. But, after buying a new stem, new handlebars and three new saddles, I began to think I'd just bought the wrong bike.

How did you gain confidence cycling?
I'm a native New Yorker and I love tours that teach, so I nervously signed up for a bike tour. I started with a tour covering the history of the Manhattan street grid, which took me from 14th Street to 126th Street via 8th Avenue and through Central Park – and that single day knocked the fear of street-riding right out of me. I followed that with loads more tours, including the moment I'm most proud of: the first leg of the New York Century Bike Tour. I only did the Central Park to Prospect Park leg for beginners, but, for this beginner, who had been terrified to ride in traffic, it was a huge milestone!

How did you cement your cycle style?
I love bike blogs that celebrate biking as part of daily life and, while I've finally found the clothes that are comfy and sweat friendly, I hate the thought of looking like the jock that I'm not. But I love the accessories: the Knog blinders, the Topeak trunk, the CatEye computer. I also cast an envious eye at the bike blogs that celebrate those pretty bikes, those Dutch bikes, those vintage bikes.

What bike do you ride now?
In an unearthed Christmas photo, I saw my 1974 Raleigh three-speed sitting under the tree. My parents had given it to me when I was 12 with the promise that it came with a lifetime guarantee. I pulled it out of a closet and wheeled it to the nearest bike shop to see what it would take to make it rideable

— and pretty. They promised to replace the tyres and cables, but insisted that the paint job and frame were just fine. I bought myself a Brooks honey-coloured leather saddle and matching grips. And a wireless Knog computer.

It looks lovely and rides beautifully. And now I have my rugged bike and my pretty bike. I don't regret the purchase of the mountain

bike because it did allow me to overcome street-riding fears. And now that New York has the CitiBike bike-share programme, I commute from work every night. Without fear. And wearing office attire — pants, loafers, skirts!

I've come a long way — my bike story has led to an involvement in the biking community that I never anticipated, and I love to share it!

7

How to . . .
Cycle in style

It is my strong belief that one of the most powerful ways to encourage more women on to bikes is by embracing the link between cycling and fashion. In a bid to do just that, this chapter offers fashion inspiration as well as practical tips, and will hopefully show that cycle clothing isn't just about Lycra.

There was a time when I wouldn't have dreamed of putting the words 'cycling' and 'fashion' in the same sentence. And here I am, several years later, running a business and writing a chapter of a book based on the harmony between the two.

I remember when I first felt the tremors of a trend, an emergent subculture bubbling under the surface . . . The problem was that cycling had become rather square. A lot of cyclists settled for an anorak, traditional helmet and sporty shorts – not the most inspiring ensemble. But, through the sea of cagoules, I would occasionally see a woman rebelliously looking feminine and stylish on her bike. *How wonderful*, I would think to myself and, after a few sightings of similarly cool creatures, I decided I wanted to join them. Once in the saddle, the elegance and style potential of cycling blew me away – looking great on your bike was both empowering and easy. It soon became clear

to me that the way to get more women cycling was to promote it as a desirable, fashionable lifestyle choice and quash the outdated image that, once in the saddle, personal taste in clothes went out the window.

But what is the essence of cycle style? Why do certain women look so resplendent riding a bike? Is it the poise of the position, the gracefulness of the glide, or is it simply that riding a bike makes you more visible than you would be just walking along a crowded street or travelling in a car?

Whatever the specific ingredients, what it boils down to is . . . WEARING AN OUTFIT YOU LOVE WHILE RIDING A BIKE YOU LOVE, ROCKS!

After a dig around online, it became abundantly clear that I was not the first to be inspired by this modern resurgence of bicycle cool. There were a handful of bloggers and designers

exploring this world and quite a network of cycle-style movers and shakers was emerging. The Cycle Chic blogs started first with Copenhagen Cycle Chic; today there are hundreds of similar blogs all over the world. The premise is simple – to post pictures of people looking cool and stylish on their bikes. The popularity of this simple format demonstrates the power of the bicycle not only as a mode of transport but as a style statement. Sometimes intentional, sometimes not, the bike is both an extension of the rider's look and a platform on which to display it.

Very quickly, cycle fashion-shows popped up, along with trend features in magazines. Fashion industry heavyweights, such as Paul Smith, Vivienne Westwood, Agyness Deyn and Elle Macpherson, showed signs of approval and love for the humble bicycle. And there was a surge of advertising and branding incorporating bicycles to portray companies as being hip and on trend.

Meanwhile, I was setting up and running Cyclechic.co.uk; our mission: to promote cycling as a desirable, accessible lifestyle choice to encourage more women to take to two wheels. And it was wonderful to see our customer base grow and see how this connection with fashion helped to shift women's opinions on cycling. A few years along and I now consider 'stylish cycling' a movement rather than a trend, as it shows no sign of fading away. And as long as women like fashion and appreciate the benefits of cycling, I am confident it will continue to flourish.

SAN FRANCISCO STYLE

Some of the finest cycle style bloggers come from San Francisco. Despite the insane hills, this spellbinding city has a vibrant, welcoming cycling community, which I have been lucky enough to visit. Who better to call upon to share some cycle style secrets?

Kirstin Tieche,
velovogue.blogspot.com
My fave outfit to cycle in would have to be one of my Diane Von Furstenberg dresses. Every time I wear one of her patterns and designs, I feel so uber-womanly! And then coupling that feeling with being on a bike brings the wow factor to an entirely new level.

Meli Burgueño, bikesandthecity.blogspot.com

I dress normally. I don't necessarily 'dress' to go on my bike, I suppose. I love fashion, I love colours and I am not afraid to show my roots and culture through my clothes with wicked patterns, the biggest hoop earrings and crazy tights/leggings. But if I'm getting dressed, or shopping for new clothes, I always do the invisible bicycle dance, just to make sure I can pedal OK.

Christina Torres, citygirlrides.com

My favourite cycling outfit would be a high-waisted skirt, light material shirt and flats. I prefer skirts that are high waisted for coverage but sit just above the knee. In warm summer climates, I tend to go for summer dresses in light materials with Spandex shorts for coverage underneath. Leggings and Spandex shorts are life savers in dresses and skirts in any season; plus, having a colourful assortment keeps it exciting.

Melissa Davies, bikepretty.com

I almost always dress for my destination. Only if I'm going further than eight miles do I dress for the ride. My uniform in San Francisco is skinny jeans, a cropped motorcycle jacket, some kind of cool top and high-heeled boots. And I always bike in heels. I only wear flats if I'm forced to go somewhere without bike access (how horrible!). I'm constantly sharing tips on my blog, BikePretty.com. Here's a tip I use all the time: if you're dressed warm enough for the first ten minutes of your ride, then you're overdressed and you'll get sweaty. Pack the coat in your pannier and arrive feeling fresh.

THE VINTAGE CONNECTION

As women have enjoyed cycling for over 100 years, it's no surprise that there is a link between vintage clothes and bicycles. Long before stretchy sportswear existed, women cycled in their own clothes, promenading the fashions of the day. There are many examples in cycling's rich history of women looking supremely elegant on their bikes – from Hollywood stars to suffragettes. Here are a few of my favourite vintage outfits that work a treat on the bike today, and are still very much seen about town. They work because they look great, yes, but also because they are practical to cycle in.

'I bought an old red bicycle with the words Free Spirit written across its side – which is exactly what I felt like when I rode it down the street in a tie-dyed dress.'
Drew Barrymore, American actress, b.1975

Pedal pushers

They ain't called pedal pushers for nothing – the cropped length is ideal for cycling, to prevent any chain chaffing or entanglements. Originally designed specifically for cycling, they became a huge fashion hit in the 1950s as women appreciated a stylish, casual alternative to the full skirts and dresses of the period. They were often high-waisted and worn with a shirt or top that was tied at the waist to show off the womanly shape. Film stars like Grace Kelly and Audrey Hepburn were partial to these cropped pants, which added to their allure, and they are still a firm favourite today. They have certainly been a staple in my wardrobe for as long as I can remember. Whether it's cropped skinny jeans with plimsolls or high-waisted capri pants with a blouse, their practicality makes these inspired trousers a keeper.

The 1920s dropped waist

A dress with a dropped waist (or no waist at all) is very comfy to cycle in. I have a 1920s style tea dress that comes out every summer and is a dream to cycle in. The lack of restriction around the waist means it's comfy and stays cool, and the skirt is usually around knee length, which means it behaves rather well when cycling. Teamed with a cloche hat to keep the sun out of your eyes and your sleek bob in place, this *Great Gatsby* look is a sheer bicycle delight that still looks great today.

The 1940s tweed suit

During the Second World War, women needed practical outfits as they were often taking on men's jobs and were very physically active, but they also needed to look feminine

and respectable – and the tweed suit fit the bill. OK, so you may not wear the whole ensemble just out and about these days, but as separate items they are brilliant on the bike. Tweed is an ideal fabric for outdoor activities and was often used for sportswear before more modern fabrics emerged – it's made from woven wool and wool is breathable but warm. It's also very durable and does not absorb water, so raindrops roll off. A knee-length tweed skirt is great for cycling and the heaviness of the fabric prevents it from flaring up in the breeze – I have a tweed skirt that I often wear to meetings when I want to be smart and cycle. A tailored tweed jacket is also an ideal cycling partner: warm, comfy and flattering, with a brightly coloured scarf and skinny jeans, it's just the thing for a crisp autumn morning,

The 1950s dress

Culottes

During the 1950s, women started wearing more playful, fun clothes and the ultra-feminine look was in. Day dresses had fitted bodices and full, wide skirts and came just below the knee (called ballerina length). Feminine, flattering and pretty as a peach, but good for cycling in? Yes, actually. The skirt is usually a good length for cycling, as long as you have a chain guard. It's light and breezy, so ideal for summer cycling, and did I mention it's pretty? Cycling in this type of dress will make you feel great and will turn heads. Simplified versions of the 1950s dress come out in the shops every summer; there may be slight tweaks here and there but the basics are the same – tailored bodice and full skirt. I have a modern version I bought in H&M a few years back and I get it out every summer on the bike. The skirt puffs out as you ride, which is ultra girly and always make me smile.

Culottes are a simplified form of the original divided skirts and became popular in France in the 1920s. The idea is that they give the illusion of being a skirt but have separate legs so give you a bit more freedom. These days, you can buy a broad range of culottes, from more casual styles to smart pairs which are ideal for the office.

The 1960s miniskirt >>>

The swinging sixties were all about freedom and youthful energy, and the cheeky miniskirt was synonymous with the times. Style icons from Twiggy to Susannah York were pictured whizzing around town on their bikes while showing off their pins in the latest fashion. But it's not just a look reserved for actresses and models, the right miniskirt can be quite freeing and comfortable to cycle in. So, if you fancy getting your legs out, then you've got nothing to lose.

CYCLE-FRIENDLY FASHION

Cycling in your regular clothes is liberating. Abandoning the cycle-specific outfit and instead making what you already have in your wardrobe work on the bike will save you time, money and faff, and can also be lots of fun.

There are some clothes that work better than others, however. Here's my run-through of cycle-friendly fashion – clothes that look and feel great, both on and off the bike – as well as some important dos and don'ts, and tips from cycle style bloggers around the world.

TROUSERS

There is a time and a place for tracksuit bottoms, but they are not the most flattering. Luckily there is a whole world of stylish slacks out there that are comfortable to cycle in.

Style choice

Tapered and straight-legged trousers work well as they avoid contact with the chain. In warmer months, pedal pushers that taper and cut off above the ankle or three-quarter-length trousers are a good choice. Leggings are an all-year-round winner and can be worn under skirts, dresses or longer tops.

Bootcut trousers can also work well, but there is an increased chance of scuffage, so you may need some bicycle clips to rein them in. Very wide-legged trousers can be awkward when cycling and can get in the way of pedalling or even get caught in the chain. Another consideration is to look for trousers that have some space or stretch in the waist, gusset and knee, for ease of movement when pedalling.

Fabrics

Try to go for natural fibres such as cotton (jeans and cords are both made of cotton), linen or a wool mix, as they will be breathable and prevent sweat patches. Also look for trousers with some elastane or Spandex in them, to give you ease of movement.

Problem-solver

If you don't want to give up your beloved bell bottoms or favourite pair of flares, but they are getting in the way as you cycle, try wearing legwarmers and tucking the trousers in well. Go for a nice, bright colour to enhance your visibility on the road.

Winter: Jeans, cords (with elastane), wool-mix trousers, leggings.

Summer: Pedal pushers (cropped trousers), three-quarter-length trousers or leggings, shorts, culottes.

'It is by riding a bicycle that you learn the contours of a country best.'
Ernest Hemingway

The cubicle test

How to be sure from the confines of a shop fitting-room cubicle that your new trousers will work for cycling. Once you've admired yourself in the mirror, adopt a far less flattering pose: bend your knees, hold on to some imaginary handlebars, ensure your curtain is pulled tight shut, and do your very best bicycling mime. If you experience any of the following, those trousers may have to go back on the peg:

1. Obtrusive seams in the gusset dig in where you would really rather they did not.
2. Top button is fine when standing but during your bicycle mime feels ready to pop.
3. Bending your knee feels like an effort and, if you persist, something is going to split.
4. You get builder's bum.
5. You can see your pants through the fabric when stretched – popular with lorry drivers but not a good look.

TOPS

Loose-fitting tops, shirts and blouses work really well for everyday cycling, and you can layer them up, depending on the weather. For figure-hugging tops, go for washable, breathable fabrics.

Boob watch

If you are wearing a tight, low-cut top, make sure your boobs stay in position – popping out while pedalling can be mortifying. If this problem persists, try a sports bra to keep your boobs in check. Also, be aware that, in the cycling position, you may be giving people a particularly good view of your cleavage. This might be intentional if you are in a flirty mood, but if you'd rather not flaunt it, perhaps sport a less revealing top or cover with another layer when cycling.

Style choice

Blouses are often made of light, breathable fabrics, cut for the female figure. They drape well and flatter without being tight and restrictive. A blouse teamed with your favourite jeans is simple, sophisticated, and versatile. Avoid dry-clean-only blouses, though; they will cost you the price of the top after two or three cleans.

Fabrics

Go for washable, breathable fabrics, like cotton, viscose or bamboo mixes; if the top is tight, look for some elastane in the mix, for ease of movement.

Problem-solver

You want to keep warm when it's cold outside but you don't want to start sweating once you've picked up a little pace. The answer to this problem is a merino-wool top. Merino wool comes from a particular breed of sheep and it naturally regulates your body temperature. It keeps the warm air, created by your body, in against your skin when you are cold but, when you have heated up, it releases hot air to keep you cool. It also absorbs sweat, taking it away from your body so you don't get sweat patches And it's also a natural antimicrobial – this basically means it will not get as smelly as a regular top after being subjected to sweat. Lastly, they look really nice on: the fabric is soft and flattering and they stretch but don't lose their shape. I have a merino-wool top that belonged to my mum in the 1980s. It's super-retro and I have worn it for all sorts of activities over the years, from cycling to dancing, hiking and skiing, and it's still going strong. If you don't have one in your wardrobe already, I would recommend you invest. (Brands: Vulpine, Swrve.)

Winter: It's all about layers. Merino-wool long-sleeved base layers, followed by shirt or blouse, light woollen jumpers and cardigans. The more layers the better, so you can adjust, depending on your body temperature.

Summer: Spaghetti-strap or sleeveless tops made of cotton or, even better, bamboo, loose shirts or blouses.

DRESSES & SKIRTS

Cycling in a dress or skirt can be both cooling and comfortable as well as feeling fantastically feminine.

Style choice

Avoid dresses with very tight, stiff bodices or restrictive arms and shoulders. Instead, look at Empire-line cuts that come in under the bust rather than cutting in at the waist, or tunics and smocks. Lengthwise, around the knee works well and shorter lengths can look great, although you might want to wear shorts or leggings underneath. Avoid long, flowing skirts that can get caught up in the spokes, chain and pedals, and might get torn or even cause an accident. Avoid pencil or other very tight, restrictive skirts with no stretch which limit leg movement.

Problem-solver

A long skirt can be pulled to the side and secured with a hairband or clothes peg to keep it out of harm's reach or stop it blowing up. You can also get bike-specific garters from US company BirdIndustries. The garter goes around your thigh and then a metal clip holds your skirt in place.

Winter: Woollen tunics or jumper dresses matched with warm woolly tights or leggings. Tweed, cord and denim skirts for warmth; just be sure they are not too tight around your legs.

Summer: Flaunt your summer dresses on the bike. Go for loose, floaty knee-length numbers that let air circulate, and enjoy the breeze against your skin. If you're worried about the wind blowing the skirt of your dress a little too high, wear three-quarter-length leggings underneath or cycling shorts that can quickly be removed when you get to your destination.

Warning

Leggings are often regarded as default cycling attire – our reliable, stretchy friends. But do double check that the material doesn't stretch to the point of being transparent when you're on the saddle, or you could be in for a knicker-flashing ride. Test them out in front of a mirror by adopting your cycling position and looking at your reflection over your shoulder. Go for leggings with thicker material or wear a long tunic over the top.

'The bicycle will accomplish more for women's sensible dress than all the reform movements that have ever been waged.'
Demorest's Family Magazine, 1895

SHOES

Shoes need to be comfy and practical both for cycling and for stopping, mounting and dismounting. It is also essential that they stay on your feet so you don't lose a shoe as you cycle. And you need a strong enough sole, so that the pedals don't dig into your feet (particularly if you use the spikier metal pedals).

Can you cycle in heels?

While I'm not sure six-inch stilettos are the ideal cycling shoe, there is no reason why you shouldn't cycle in heels. A small heel need not get in the way of pedalling. When stopping at lights, I have found a small, wide heel quite useful to get the supporting foot into a stable position quickly. And as you don't have the pressure of your whole body weight on your feet when riding a bike, heels are certainly comfier to cycle in than they are to walk in.

Style choice

Thank goodness brogues are now as popular for women as they are for men! It's a great shoe for cycling: comfortable and sturdy, but sophisticated – a timeless classic. These days, you can also get ladies' brogues with a nice heel and find a great assortment of colours.

Flip-flops might be a nice idea for summer cycling but it's not so nice when they flip themselves into the middle of the road mid-cycle. Try sandals with a heel strap instead. Ballet shoes can also be a touch temperamental – if opting for these, try to go for a leather pair instead of plastic, as they will have more staying power. Wedges can be a good summer shoe to cycle in and will give you some height when off the bike, but you may have to raise your saddle slightly if you cycle in them regularly, as a chunky wedge will affect your cycling position.

Winter: Leather boots work wonders for warmth and keeping trousers tucked in.

Summer: Sandals with toe, heel and ankle support, plimsolls, deck shoes.

Melissa Davies, San Francisco >>>

My best friend from fashion school instilled in me a love of brogues, or wing-tips as we call them in America. I found this heeled pair in a pay-by-weight charity shop and had them fixed up. I love how they pull an outfit together. I also own a pair of Ferragamo brogues that I brought with me while travelling. When I visited my friends in London, we were like a little stylish cycling club. And every one of us was wearing a pair of brogues!

COATS AND JACKETS

Whether it's a coat to keep you cosy in the winter or the perfect waterproof jacket, suitable outerwear is essential for year-round cycling. Cycling jackets make lots of sense and there are some stylish options out there (see box on page 156). But it is totally doable to cycle year-round without a cycle-specific jacket. Your jacket will often be the main part of your outfit on show when cycling, so don't feel you have to sacrifice style and zip yourself into a coat you would never usually wear.

Winter: **Wool-mix coats** are great for winter cycling as they are warm yet have

natural stretch and breathability and can take light showers.

Autumn: A lightweight **leather jacket** has lots of benefits for the cyclist. Leather is very durable and warm and will protect you from wind or rain but will also limit sweating.

Summer: Cotton **blazers** are great for spring and summer cycling. Look for blazers that have some elastane in the fabric for ease of movement, or go for a looser, boyfriend fit. A washable blazer is the perfect jacket for cycling to work or other smart engagements.

Spring: A **classic mac** is often made of treated cotton or microfibre, and is

breathable and water-resistant. The longer length can keep your legs dry or you can undo the buttons if you'd rather get some air circulating. Traditional macs with a smart collar and belted waist have a 1940s elegance that works a treat on a bicycle. Many high-street shops bring in a range of macs in early spring; otherwise, have a hunt in charity shops or look at eBay for vintage versions.

Capes

A cape can be an ideal alternative to a coat for a cyclist. They don't restrict your back or shoulders when cycling and don't cling to the body, so you stay well ventilated. Go for a cape with armholes, so you can put your hands through to reach the handlebars. A nice wool or tweed cape can be perfect for spring and autumn cycling. If it's chilly, ensure you have a warm, long-sleeved top on underneath and good gloves.

You can get cycle-specific rain capes made from breathable fabrics, the front of which is designed to sit over your handlebars so it creates a protective cover, keeping your legs completely shielded. They have thumb hooks so you can secure the cape and keep your hands on the handlebars. However, a cape will be anything but aerodynamic and if it's very windy it may be difficult to get on and keep in place. Nevertheless, they have become a favourite with urban cyclists who prefer style over speed.

Cycle-specific coats and jackets

Cycle-specific coats for women have come on in leaps and bounds in recent years. There are now some great fashion-forward options that take function and form into account in equal measure.

Cyclodelic

Urban Legend

Georgia in Dublin

Ana Nichoola

CYCLING IN THE RAIN

I'm not going to lie to you: cycling in the rain (and not getting wet) requires a little thought and planning. Invariably, when you leave the house there's not a cloud in the sky; it's the freak downpour on the way home that catches you out, so you need to be prepared.

If you don't wear a cycle-specific coat, it's a good idea to have a lightweight waterproof on you at all times. Go for a rain cape, mac or poncho that folds away neatly into its own pouch so you can whip it out when the rain starts to fall and stow it away easily once you get to your destination. That way, you can wear your regular coat and just put the cape or poncho on if it starts to rain.

Regular anoraks and waterproof macs can work well for short journeys, especially if they have long skirts to keep your legs dry too. But waterproof macs made of rubber or polyester do not breathe well and will get sweaty if picking up pace on longer trips.

If you have a waist-length anorak, you may want to opt for waterproof trousers. Not the sleekest look ever, but you will have total coverage and ease of movement. Or you could look at more fashion-forward options such as waterproof boot covers and wraps from Georgia in Dublin

Although it might be tempting to wear your 'comfort' jacket, with its large fluffy hood, and pull it over your head to block out the miserable, rainy world, don't. Hoods – the bigger and fluffier, the worse – can seriously affect your peripheral vision, causing you to miss traffic. Go for a peaked helmet with fewer or no ventilation holes to stop the rain from going in your eyes and to keep your luscious locks dry.

If you don't have full coverage over your legs in the rain, avoid jeans. Denim is a heavy fabric and it takes a long time to dry. It's no fun facing a day with soggy jeans, when your attempts to lift your thighs up to the hand-dryer have failed, after that unexpected morning shower on the way in. Try wool-mix trousers or lighter trousers or leggings.

Shoe-wise, you can't beat long leather boots. They will not absorb water and the length will prevent rain from creeping into your socks.

THE LAZY CYCLIST
Forget it!

If it's chucking it down in the morning, take a break from the bike. Bust out your wellies and umbrella instead, and have a cup of tea on the train.

PROFILE

Georgia Scott, founder of Georgia in Dublin

Website: georgiaindublin.com

What was the inspiration for Georgia in Dublin?

When we first started in December 2009, we could find no attractive rainwear that was designed specifically with the female urban cyclist in mind. Plastic bags seemed to be the only option for keeping your shoes and trouser-ends dry in a downpour and you had to bunch a skirt up around your waist to get waterproof trousers on. There had to be a better alternative! We have therefore designed elegant yet highly functional products that accommodate normal everyday clothing, look good on and off the bike and create for the wearer a blissful (or, dare we say, smug!) sense of indifference to inclement weather!

Can you recommend good clothes to wear under your rainwear, on the bike?

The idea with the Georgia in Dublin range is that you are not restricted in terms of what you choose to wear underneath, both in terms of style and comfort. You can wear as much as you need to in winter, next to nothing in summer and whatever takes your fancy for an evening out! The Dublette, for example, is an elegant jacket that is designed to expand over several layers of bulky clothing or even a backpack, but is the perfect shell layer in warmer temperatures.

If you are wearing several layers, a base garment with good wicking is advisable.

What are the key things to look for in waterproofs for cycling?

Although the level of waterproofing is obviously very important, breathability is also key. You also want a fit that accommodates the movement of a cyclist on whatever type of bike they may be using.

What do you wear to cycle in on a sunny day?

Well, unfortunately, we don't tend to see enough of those in Ireland, but when we do Nickie (the 'senior' partner!) tends to wear T-shirt-style jersey dresses and I generally make the most of it and don a pretty, full-skirted summer dress (skirt guards are a great idea but the Rainwrap also tames and contains any float-away fabric). My Dorothy cover is always there to protect the contents of my generally overfilled basket [see right] from hopping out.

What do you love about cycling?

We both love the flexibility and the lack of restrictions associated with cycling. You can go wherever you like, whenever you like, without having to worry about getting stuck in traffic. My bike has no gears, so it keeps me fit tootling around Dublin and I find I do my best thinking and enjoy the time alone when I'm cycling. Also, it's free (when I was a student, I saved a fortune on taxi fares), it's easy and there are no negative implications for the environment, which is important to us.

CYCLING IN THE DARK

Traditional high-visibility gear has a reputation for being ugly and dorky. This presents a problem for women who want to be safe and visible but don't want an entire extra wardrobe of Day-Glo clothes.

The simple, high-visibility belt is a good option if you don't fancy being fluorescent from head to toe. It goes across the shoulder and fastens around the waist (look at brands like TWO n FRO and Retro Reflectives for more attractive versions than the standard yellow strip). You can simply pop these on over your regular coat and they will give you a great reflective element across your body, viewable from front and back. A more feminine version is a reflective sash; made of reflective fabric, these slip on across your shoulder and accomplish the mean feat of being fun and reflective.

You could team a belt or sash with reflective ankle straps – the ankles being an ideal place to wear a reflective item as they are in view of drivers from all angles, and, as they move with pedalling, they are more likely to catch a driver's eye than your body or arm. You can either get the type of ankle straps that snap to close and curl around your ankle or the type that fasten with velcro. They're also great for taming bootcut trousers.

You can get a whole host of stylish reflective accessories that can look great day and night, including helmet bows, badges, brooches, scarves, hats, and even shoe tassels.

Make it at home

If you have a coat with a detachable belt, buy a strip of reflective ribbon or tape (available on eBay and very inexpensive) and then sew it on to one side of your belt. Then, you can flip your belt over when cycling at night, and it will shine like a beacon for traffic behind.

Bright sparks

Two companies have taken the problem of ugly high-viz clothing and turned it into an opportunity.

<<< Dashing Tweeds

This British company have developed a method of weaving a reflective twill into tweed and woollen fabrics. The result is incredibly smart, tailored outfits and woollen accessories that look wonderful by day and glow by night. Dashing Tweeds do a range of tweed suits, jackets and capes, hats, legwarmers and even dog coats, and have collaborated with stalwart brands like Converse, Brooks and Topshop.

<<< Haute Réflecture by Vespertine

An American brand creating extremely feminine reflective-wear. In fact, some items resemble underwear, with rather sensual-looking vests and camisole tops. They may be a bit racy for some, but they also do macs and waistcoats that are more substantial and a pleasant change from shapeless jackets.

Sarah Carton, half-English and half-Swedish, lives and cycles in Stockholm, Sweden

It's often below zero in Stockholm so you have to be prepared. My outfit starts with thermals in bamboo or merino wool to keep the wind out. Thermal knickers are also good as they keep your bum warm. Levi's Demi Curve jeans are nice and stretchy, and I can wear my thermals underneath. My coat is a Gloverall duffel. It's really warm and easy to unbutton if I get hot while riding. On my feet I wear Blundstone boots. They are Australian work boots, similar to Chelsea boots. They are made out of leather with a rubber sole: really sturdy, warm enough for winter and pretty much waterproof. I always wear a hat under my helmet and a warm pair of gloves and a huge woolly scarf. And, for the bike, it's vital you have winter tyres – it's the only thing that will keep you upright in the ice and snow.

COLOURS AND COORDINATION

Wearing bright colours on your bike not only makes you stand out from the crowd but can also be a useful visibility aid. Accessory-wise, brightly coloured helmets can ensure you are spotted from quite some distance and brightly coloured panniers are great at making you visible to traffic from behind.

ACCESSORIZE!

Sunglasses

This one is pretty simple, really: if the sun is in your eyes and hindering your view of the road, get your sunglasses on. If you are wearing a helmet, check it's comfortable to wear with sunglasses, and be sure they are tight enough and won't fall off. As well as performing their primary function, sunglasses can prevent bugs or dust going in your eyes as you ride. If you want to go for cycle-specific sunglasses, there are plenty out there and they are designed to stay on and be light and comfy, and some have interchangeable lenses for different light conditions. For an attractive pair of sunglasses aimed at the active girl, check out Oakley's Backhand sunnies. They come in a range of colours and have glamorous 1970s-style frames but are lightweight and designed to stay in place when exercising.

Scarves

Scarves are great for all seasons to stop cold wind rushing down your neck, but it's very important to tie or tuck them in securely and not to leave the ends trailing. The wind can easily blow scarves off and that could lead to a cold neck, a lost scarf and even an accident. You could look at a circular scarf, snood or neck warmer to avoid this potential problem.

Hats

A nice warm hat that stays on securely when you cycle can be a godsend for winter cycling. If you wear a helmet, you may be able to get a slim-fitting hat on underneath that will stop the cold air creeping in the ventilation holes and keep your precious ears warm. Some helmets also come with winter ear warmers that attach to the helmet.

If you're not a helmet-wearer, go for something toasty that will not get blown off in the wind; ensure it covers your ears but doesn't affect your peripheral vision. It doesn't need to be cold to don a hat on your bike, though; a hat can be great to protect your hair and head from the wind and can give you a certain panache – as long as it stays on!

Top tip: Berets look rather ravishing on a bike but that jaunty position means they can easily get swept off in the wind. Try using hair clips to keep it in place so you can carry off your Parisian look without losing your hat!

PROFILE
Zsófi Geréby, Budapest, founder
of urban-cyclewear brand Urban
Legend
Website: urbanlegend.cc

What bike do you ride and why?
I ride an old and slightly rusty 1980s road
bike by the name of Rothmann. He is red
and all his components are original Shimano
Dura Ace. We've been through six years
of tough urban commute together – he is
fast, reliable and a real survivor. Also, as he
looks so tired and worn out, I can leave him
anywhere. Only I know his hidden treasures.

What's the cycle scene like in
Budapest?
I was born in Budapest and I have lived here
ever since. I've cycled every day since I was
18, day and night, summer and winter. The
cycling culture in Budapest is a self-made one;
ten years ago, only crazy people and bike

messengers were on the road. Ever since
the Critical Mass movement started to grow,
more and more people realized cycling is the
only enjoyable way of transportation. With
very little governmental help, now more than
18 per cent of the city population use bikes
every day. I have high hopes for us becoming
a real cycling capital in a few years.

How are the roads in your city?
There's been a tremendous change in drivers'
attitudes in the past few years. There are
still a few 'misunderstandings' but now both
parties accept they are not the only users of
the roads. Yes, I feel safe now.

What's your favourite outfit to
cycle in?
As a (bicycle) fashion designer, I have a
carefully picked wardrobe with completely
'normal' looks, but I can wear every piece
on the bike. I wear most of my own designs,
partly to try them out, to test them, partly
because my original goal of founding
Urban Legend was to design weatherproof
garments that look great on and off the bike.

What was the inspiration behind
Urban Legend?
Urban Legend is the first Hungarian fashion
label specializing in urban bike apparel. It
was inspired by my own experiences as
a supporter of urban cycling. As a regular
Budapest cyclist, I often pondered about the
ideal way to dress for biking around the city
year-round. Urban Legend thus was born out
of personal experience, do-it-yourself craft
and openness towards creative solutions.

8

How to . . .
Cycle to work

Whether it's avoiding the congestion of public transport or injecting fresh air and exercise into your daily routine, cycling to work can truly brighten up the daily grind. If you need a little encouragement to get you started, this chapter covers everything from planning the route to suggestions for what to eat for breakfast and tips on combating helmet hair!

On the brink of biking in?

You've been considering cycling to work for a while. On a sunny day, you've envied a carefree cyclist as you're stuck on a bus, descending underground or rushing to catch a train. You promise yourself you will look into it but, once you get to work, the business of the day ensues and you never quite get around to getting on your bike.

I totally hear you . . . I did this for about six months and would kick myself every day on my journey to work for still not having taken any action. But you don't just fall into cycling to work. Decisions have to be made and strategic planning is necessary. You will need to make some time, perhaps over a couple of weekends, to get yourself organized and make sure you realize your goal.

If you need a little encouragement to push you over the brink and on to your bike,

here's what some women say they love about cycling to work:

- 'I love that I can travel on my timescale, and I don't have to rely on public transport. When cycling to work, it wakes me up in the morning and, when coming home, it winds me down from the day.' (Menna Jenkins, London)
- 'As a business owner, cycling allows me to cram so much more into my day, as I am in complete control of my travel time and cycling gives me the energy to work harder!' (Amy Fleuriot, founder of Cyclodelic, London)
- 'Cycling to work takes me eight minutes and means I can pop home in my breaks. There are queues of traffic in the morning and I just whizz past them all, laughing! Cycling to work means exercise and transport combined.' (Lynne Collinson, Southsea)
- 'No matter if I feel grumpy or lazy, I start to smile and feel happy once I'm on a bike. It expanded my area of work as well.

Nowadays, I write about bike topics from London for a cycling magazine in Japan, which is great fun.' (Miki Yamanouchi, London/Japan)

- 'I cycle to work every day, unless it is raining heavily or snowing. I find it peaceful. I sing to myself as I go. I am far away from the smell, noise, pickpocketing and hustle-bustle of commuters on public transport.' (Estelle Jobson, Switzerland/South Africa)

OK, now you are ready and raring to go, here's a step-by-step guide to ensure it really happens.

Get your bike ready to go

The essential first step is, of course, getting a bike that you like to ride and that's fit for the job. If you've not got your set of wheels sorted yet, take a look at *Find a bike you like* (p22). Or, if you have a bike that's not been ridden for a while and you need to get it ready for action, check out *Maintain your bike* (p74). Put some time aside for either option.

Build up your confidence

If you've not cycled for a while, it may be overly ambitious to start commuting straight away. Start with a few local trips, go out on your bike with friends, perhaps take a cycling lesson to get yourself to a stage where you are confident on the road.

Plan your route

Don't just set off on a Monday morning with a vague idea of where you're going, hoping for the best. You could get lost – which is both stressful, if you're late for work, and exhausting, if you're new to cycling. Have a good look at the route from the comfort of your home – I usually consult the cycle directions on Google Maps. Or you may find that there is a good map of your local area or city with specific cycle routes and cycle lanes highlighted – these may be paper maps or online facilities, or even smartphone apps. Check with your transport network or local authority, or have a hunt online.

Do a practice run

Armed with maps or the route on your phone, choose a day when you have no time restraints and test out the journey. Perhaps make a day of it, taking a mate with you and stopping off along the way for a coffee

Workplace cycle schemes

In the UK, check if you're eligible for the Cycle to Work scheme. If your employer has signed up to the government scheme, they essentially loan you the money to purchase a brand-new bike. You then pay this back monthly from your salary over a period of 12 or 18 months – this is known as a salary sacrifice. As the money comes out of your wages, you do not pay tax on it, nor do you have to fork out the cost in one go.

or some lunch. Take time to get to know your route – you may discover a convenient alleyway that doesn't show up on the map, or a cute café where you can get your morning croissant. Note down road names and landmarks, even take quick snaps on your phone – anything that will help you familiarize yourself with the route. It will also help you to suss out confusing infrastructure and junctions, so you know what you're doing when you take that first workday trip.

Choose the right day

For me, it was a crisp, sunny Tuesday morning in March. Early spring is my favourite time of year and I love being outdoors. Monday mornings are not good for me but on Tuesdays I am usually buzzing with optimism and energy. A sunny Tuesday in March is not a hard and fast rule, but the point is to choose a day when you feel positive and excited about your new venture. Whatever day it is, when it comes, make sure you set out early so that you have plenty of time – you don't want to feel rushed and there may be factors you didn't expect that add time to your journey (traffic, needing to stop for a drink, finding parking etc).

THE ROUTE

Trial and error

Don't be afraid to experiment with your route; however, my advice would be to do this on the way home, not on the way into work. In a whimsical mood one morning, I got tempted down a pretty road, convinced

it would be a shortcut. I got further and further away from anything I recognized but was too stubborn to admit defeat. I carried on until the road eventually came to a dead end at a noisy cement works and I ended up very, very late for work. Lesson learned. But, on the positive side, my experimenting (after work) eventually paid off and I found a perfect route that cut out many of the major thoroughfares and took me down pretty tree-lined streets that made me smile every day.

Bike buddy

Find a more experienced commuter who lives near you and see if you can cycle with them on the way in or way home. Get chatting to fellow cyclists in the office or look online for organized bike-buddy rides from your area into the heart of the city.

What's a good distance to cycle?

Obviously, an appropriate journey length will depend very much on your fitness level, speed and personal preference. But here's a rough guide:

1–3 miles: This is a nice cycle ride, very doable every day and a good distance for beginners. It's also unlikely that any other form of transport will get you there any quicker – which is very satisfying.

3–5 miles: This might feel like a bit of a push if you're just starting out, but it is still very doable. You may want to do one day on, one day off, when getting closer to five miles.

5–10 miles: You will need to have a good level of fitness, but it's totally doable. Start by doing it once a week and you will soon notice your stamina and fitness improve. You can then make it more frequent when your body gets used to it, and you'll be as fit as a fiddle a month or so in.

10+ miles: This is pretty hardcore, but many people do cycle this kind of distance, so if you are up for it, go for it! You will need to build up to it and ensure you do not wear yourself out, especially if you have an active job sandwiched in the middle. A road bike would help but it is not essential, and your bottom will thank you for investing in a pair of padded shorts.

MINIMIZE FAFF

Wouldn't it be nice if we could just click our fingers and suddenly we were fully kitted out, bag packed and loaded on board, and cycling merrily along to work, and then, when we arrived, with another click the bike was securely parked up and we were getting on with our working day? Unfortunately, unless your name is Mary Poppins, this is never going to happen, so the best you can do is make the transition as smooth and faff-free as possible.

Plan your wardrobe in advance

You will need to put some thought into what you are going to wear. Ideally, you want an outfit that will work both on and off the bike unless your journey is a long one and you

can shower and change upon arrival. The main things to consider are comfort, ease of movement and the weather. Take a look at *Cycle in style* (p138) for a more detailed analysis of what to wear on your bike.

Choose the right luggage

Make sure you know in advance what luggage you're going to be using, and check you can carry everything you need safely and comfortably while cycling. A rucksack or messenger bag will do fine to start off with, but you may want to graduate to panniers when taking laptops or heavier loads. This will put less strain on your back and shoulders and won't interfere with your riding at all, as some shoulder bags can. See 'Bags, baskets and panniers' in *Accessorize your ride* (p58).

Tips for transporting laptops

- Leave a spare power cable at the office. This will save you wrestling with wires twice a day and will make your load lighter too.
- Always put your laptop in a padded and waterproof sleeve before you put it in your pannier or bag. You don't want your beloved getting bumped and rained on as you cycle.

- You can get panniers and rucksacks with safe, secure and sometimes padded laptop compartments. Go on – give your laptop a little luxury.

Be prepared

Pack for all eventualities – but do it in advance! You may need:

- **Spare inner tube**
If you get a puncture on your way to work, you don't want to be doing a full puncture repair at the side of the road. Learn how to change the inner tube (see 'How to mend punctures' in *Maintain your bike*, p95) and always carry a spare inner tube with you.

- **Waterproofs and lights**
You may have left the house in glorious sunshine, but by home time it's pouring with rain. If your regular coat is not waterproof, keep some form of waterproof in your pannier or bag; a lightweight mac, cape or poncho that can be folded up small is ideal. You should also always carry lights, either on your bike or in your bag/pannier, so you don't get caught out if the rain clouds gather or you decide to work late.

- **Food and drink**
This may not be necessary for a short commute but, for anything over three miles, I would recommend taking a bottle of water and perhaps a snack. You may feel fine when you set off, but hunger and thirst can creep up on you and be distracting.

Bikers' breakfasts

- **Granary toast and honey**
Quick, easy to prepare and tasty, as well as being packed full of slow-releasing carbs and natural sugar for energy.
- **Muesli with sliced fresh fruit**
Energy, fibre and one of your five a day: a good breakfast for your ride that will set you up until lunchtime.
- **Smoothie made from fresh fruit**
Ensure you throw some bananas in for energy. You may need some carbs once you get to work, though.
- **Poached egg on a wholewheat bagel**
Energy and protein galore!

Leaving the house

Leave your bike in a place that is easy to access in the morning. If you keep it indoors, don't leave it tucked behind a clothes rack in the spare room. If, like me, you are 50 per cent clumsier in the morning, then you don't want to be wheeling or carrying a large, heavy object past various obstacles, especially when in a rush. Leave your bike as near to the front door as you can practically get it to reduce your morning stress levels.

Locking up

Locking and unlocking your bike is an inevitable faff, so make sure you have a system in place to make it as straightforward as it can be. Ensure you have a home for your locks when they're not in use, preferably attached to the bike itself or in your basket, if you have one. Figure out your locking technique – what's the easiest (and most secure) way of feeding the lock through the bike and locking it to the stand? Don't worry if locking leaves you exasperated to start with; once you've got used to a specific lock, you finesse your moves and it does become a smoother process. Another way to lighten your load is to leave a heavy lock at work.

Parking at work

Check out the parking situation at your workplace. There may be secure bike parking, which will give you peace of mind and save you hunting around for a good spot in the mornings. If there is no specific cycle parking, talk to your boss or HR department – see if they are prepared to give up one car-parking space and install a few bike stands.

HOW TO STAY FRESH AS A DAISY

A common misconception is that, when cycling anywhere, you'll arrive at your destination hideously hot and sweaty, desperate for a shower and full change of clothes. This may be the case if you plan on speeding along for 20 miles, which is fine if there is a shower at the office, but it's by no means the rule on a regular commute. Don't be afraid to get a little out of breath – just enough to ignite a radiant glow – but avoid getting flustered or sweaty if you want to make the transition from bike to workplace as hassle free as possible.

Something to leave at home. . .

• Relegate the rucksack
A rucksack may seem like the easiest option, and certainly for your first few trips it'll be fine, but if you commute regularly, ditch it. Not only will it give you extra weight to carry, but it can also result in sore shoulders and an unpleasant sweaty back. Invest in a rack and pannier, letting the bike take the weight so you and your clothes can breathe easily. See *Accessorize your ride* (p58).

Some things to bring along for the ride . . .

• Boyfriend T-shirt
If you feel the need for a little freshen-up on arrival, cycle in a loose-fitting T-shirt and take a smarter top or blouse in your pannier or bag. Nip to the toilets for a quick change and a spritz of deodorant, and you can walk into that morning meeting with confidence. (Far easier than removing layers of tight clothing in a cramped loo.)

• Spare pair of shoes
If your office shoes just don't work on the bike, leave your smarter shoes at work

so you can do a seamless shoe-change under your desk when you get in.

• Spare pair of knickers
Comfortable, cotton knickers are a good option for cycling. On longer commutes I carry a spare pair in my pannier – a great way to feel instantly clean and fresh.

• Face wipes
Face wipes in your pannier or in your drawer at work can be a godsend for a quick freshen-up after an energetic or unexpectedly warm ride in.

• Deodorant
Just in case.

Can I cycle in make-up?

This very much depends on your personal preference, speed of cycling and weather conditions. I have never had any problems with light make-up when cycling at a gentle pace. A touch of foundation, blusher and mascara is my standard for work, and I often apply lipstick on arrival. Here are a few tips to prevent make-up mishaps:

• Watch out for panda eyes
If you have heavy mascara on and get caught in a shower or get overly sweaty, you may turn up with a somewhat scary 'Alice Cooper' look. Try waterproof mascara or a helmet with a peak that prevents the rain making contact with your face.

• Try tinted moisturizer
Tinted moisturizer can be a better option

than slapping on layers of foundation before you ride. Look for one that has built-in sunscreen, too, for those sunny days.

• Apply your make-up at work
Let your skin breathe as you cycle, then, when you get to work, simply wipe or splash with water, and put your make-up on. You may find that your skin looks better after a cycle ride, anyway – fresh air and exercise can do wonders – and you might not need so much make-up.

CITY COMMUTERS

Vicky Coy: engineer, London

The last couple of years have seen me use my bike a lot for work. I work as an engineer, and my main project has been the redevelopment of King's Cross Central in London. I am out and about a lot in my working day and have to cycle from my office to the site or to site meetings, so carry my site kit – hard hat, steel-soled boots and high-viz jacket – on my bike, all in a straw pannier. Cycling is the best way for me to get around for work; it's faster than public transport, cheap, I can park next to or outside wherever I need to be and it gives me such freedom. It's a liberator.

I ride my bike in whatever I need to be wearing for my destination. Work clothes, going-out clothes, high heels, winter coats and woolly hats. What I feel most great in is an outfit that makes a head or two turn. Blue metallic high heels are a firm favourite when I've clocked off and put my steel-soled boots away!

Adina Daar: market researcher, New York City

I cycle from my home in Brooklyn to work in SoHo every day. I used to carry fresh clothes back and forth, but ultimately learned that I am much happier when I don't have to think about it. I keep a few nice dresses and pairs of shoes in the office for client meetings, and then I stick to jeans and tops for the rest of the time. The real struggle comes when I go out after work and decide not to cycle home on a given evening. Every so often I have to do a trip on the subway to get all my stuff in the right place, but it's a small price to pay for such an awesome way of getting around.

For me, cycling represents a personal space for all of the '-tions' in life – relaxation, reflection, ideation, creation – and, in the city, it is also about adrenaline and excitement. On my bike, I make so many decisions before I even arrive at work in the morning, which makes me feel productive and successful before I sit down at my desk.

HOW TO COMBAT HELMET HAIR

The prospect of helmet hair is a worry that looms over many women and puts some off cycling altogether. Now, I am not saying my life depends on my hair, but a bad hair day can put me in a bad mood and there is no way I want to start the day with sweaty hair slapped down against my head. However, in my experience, this is very rarely the case and, having cycled in helmets for several years, I can honestly say – hand on heart – that my dignity and hairstyles have remained intact.

The key thing I have found is to have clean hair. Clean hair puts up a much harder fight and will bounce back with a bit of a shake once the helmet is removed. The other important factor is to go for a helmet with some ventilation, especially in the summer. This allows your head to breathe and prevents sweating.

Helmet tips by hairstyle

Fringes: Try sweeping a fringe gently to the side before you put your helmet on, to prevent it getting squashed to your forehead. If your fringe insists on kinking, take some travel straighteners or a heated circular brush with you, or leave them in a drawer at work. Whatever you do, don't bend it backwards from the roots, tucking it under your helmet – your fringe won't forgive you for the rest of the day.

The tousled look: Hurray for the tousled look! It's a lifesaver for those of us with wavy or curly hair. It will save you a lot of time and it doesn't need to be perfect because that's all part of the look! In the morning, blow-dry your hair roughly and apply a light product to define your waves or separate the curls. Then apply dry shampoo to the roots, which not only helps your hair fight the dreaded 'helmet flatness' but also soaks up sweat. When you remove the helmet, do a sexy hair shake, then define the waves or curls with your fingers (do not use a brush) – and you can go on your carefree, tousled way.

Hair up: If you have medium-length or long hair, wear it in a low ponytail, loose plait or scruffy low bun to stop it getting straggly from the ride. When you get to work, unleash your hair from the helmet, remove the hairband and shake it to get any helmet lines or flatness out (or maybe give it a quick brush). If it looks rubbish, simply redo the plait, ponytail or bun.

Short crops: Leave hair wet and apply leave-in conditioner. Then, when you remove your helmet, you can restyle; if you have a hand-dryer in the loos at work, stick your head under it and give it a quick blast to dry.

Head scarf: There are two ways to play it with a scarf:

1. Tie it over your hair before your ride (bandanna style) and put the helmet over the top. A silk scarf is thin so will not affect the fit of helmet and will keep your hair from frizzing – ideal for sleek, straight locks.

2. The other use of a scarf is more of an emergency tactic, for those borderline days when you really should have washed your hair but couldn't be bothered. You remove your helmet at work and see that all the life has been squashed out of your poor barnet and no amount of shaking or dry shampoo can revive it. In this situation, bundle your hair up on top of your head. Fold a square scarf over and over lengthways until you have a long strip, put it around the back of your neck and then bring it up and tie it at the top or side – a kooky style to rescue the worst case of helmet hair.

THE ARE-YOU-READY CHECKLIST

- You have a bike that you like riding and that has been fully maintenance checked.
- You've brushed up on your cycling skills and feel confident for the commute.
- You've planned your route and done a practice run.
- You have GPS on your phone or maps in your bag.
- Your luggage and accessories are organized.
- Your outfit is organized.
- You're feeling healthy and positive.

If the answer is yes to all of these, go for it!

THE LAZY CYCLIST
Give yourself a break!

Just because you have started cycling to work it doesn't mean you have to do it religiously, every day. Try one day on, one day off or just two or three days a week. Don't enforce cycling on yourself – do it because you want to, not because you feel you should.

PROFILE
Txell Hernández Gil, Barcelona
Blog: barcelonacyclechic.blogspot.com.es

What bike do you ride and why do you like it?

It depends on my mood, the things that I have to do that day, the weather, the clothes that I am wearing . . . but I usually ride one of two bikes. I love my Orbea Dude bike to move fast from one point to another, crossing the city with this cool black and bronze bike. It is very light and elegant. When I have more time, or when I wear a short dress, I prefer to ride my classic Taurus bike. It is so cute, old-school style – very girlie – especially when I put the basket on.

What city do you cycle in and what's the cycle scene/community like? How are the roads in your city – good for cycling?

I live and work in Barcelona and I've been riding here since a decade ago. At that time it was quite rare to find someone riding a bicycle here but, since the Bicing (Barcelona's bike sharing system) arrived in 2007, there are many more bikes and bike lanes. This is not Copenhagen but, little by little, people are starting to change their minds and are getting used to cycling and respecting cyclists. The good thing is that the cycling scene is growing quite fast and it is easy to find 'bike freaks' riding fixies, BMX bicycles, repairing vintage frames, etc.

How does cycling benefit your life?

I met my husband through cycling and we run a bike rental shop and a bicycle courier company. Cycling is my life, my work, my whole thing. We are expecting a baby and we will name him Eddy, after Eddy Merckx, the famous Belgian cyclist. Yes, cycling is a very important thing in my life.

What's your favourite outfit to cycle in?

I cycle wearing skirts, dresses, heels, shorts . . . everything. You just need a comfy and stylish raincoat for the rainy days, a thick scarf, gloves and hat for wintertime and light clothes to battle the hot days. Summertime in Barcelona can be very warm, so wearing a light cotton or silk dress is always a good option.

Do you cycle to work or for leisure, or both?

I always cycle. To work, to go out, to go shopping . . . Always.

9

How to . . .
Cycle for fun

Cycling is fun. Cycling is sociable. Cycling inspires people, motivates people and brings people together. Whether you just want to pop to the shops with the kids in tow, venture further afield on a bicycle holiday or dip your toe into the world of cycle events (from naked bike rides to bicycle ballet), this chapter will encourage you to get on your bike and get stuck in.

I'm amazed by the vast number of cycling events happening throughout the year and by the diverse and creative things one can get up to on a bike. In one spring week I went to a bicycle drawing class at a prestigious London museum, took my chuckling four-year-old daughter for a ride in a cargo bike at a new bike shop in the neighbourhood and watched the phenomenon that is the 'London Tweed Run' wend its way through the streets in all its vintage finery.

People are passionate about bikes and people connect through bikes – you only need to scratch a little beneath the surface and you'll find a world of rides, groups, events, activities and communities involving cycling. Whether it's a teenage girls' dirt-riding group or an architectural city tour for the over-sixties, there really is something for everyone. All you need to do is get involved.

OUT AND ABOUT

Cycling and shopping

Whether it's a leisurely pootle on a Saturday or a rushed trip to the supermarket, doing it by bicycle can be both practical and pleasurable with these tips:

• Park your bike in one place and walk from shop to shop
If you are visiting a few different shops, don't waste precious shopping time by taking your bike from shop to shop. Instead, park it securely somewhere in the middle, so you only have to lock and unlock once.

• Panniers, panniers, panniers
Using panniers will make your life so much easier. Balancing supermarket bags on your handlebars is neither safe nor elegant!

Go for single panniers that are easy to attach and detach so you can take them into the supermarket and load your groceries up straight from the till. And an emergency fold-away rucksack is always a good idea, for any impulse buys that won't fit in on top of the weekly shop.

• Mount your lock to your frame
Finding space for your lock when you are loaded up with shopping can be a problem, so invest in a D lock that comes with a frame mount.

• Order heavy stuff online
For those heavy or cumbersome items – cans, olive oil, wine – do an online shop to lighten the load.

Cycling and going out at night

Cycling when going out in the evening can be a great money-saver, and it's an exhilarating and romantic way to arrive at the theatre, cinema or for a dinner date. (Take a compact mirror with you to check on arrival for sweat, helmet hair or mud splats.) But, if you are planning on having a few drinks, the 'bar or bike' quandary must be addressed. While some boast that one advantage of cycling over driving is that you can get away with a few drinks, the question is, at what cost?

In the UK, the police can stop you if they think you are too drunk to cycle safely and, while they can't breathalyse you, if they can prove you are not in sufficient control (i.e. unfit to cycle safely), you could be faced with a charge and a hefty fine. And, in Poland, Germany, France and some US states, you can be breathalysed and prosecuted for drink-cycling just as you can for drink-driving, so be sure to doublecheck the law when travelling. But the crux of the matter is that cycling drunk on the roads is dangerous. As with driving, the key to cycle safety is being constantly alert and, if your senses are numbed by alcohol, you are prone to losing your balance or misjudging distances, and this means you are running a major risk.

Be honest with yourself before you go out: if you know you are likely to have a few drinks, leave the bike at home. Don't kid yourself that you're only going to stay for one if your track record suggests otherwise. That way, you can just relax and enjoy your night. Often, though, we are caught by surprise; one after-work drink leads to another and another. If you already have the bike with you, give yourself a one-drink rule and then make other arrangements to get home:

- Find a taxi firm that will take a bike and put the number in your phone. If you have quick-release wheels, you can take the front wheel off to make it more compact.
- Check out train routes that let you take your bike on board. Often, city trains are more lenient after rush hour.

Other safety considerations at night

- If cycling home after a night out, agree to text your friends to tell them you got home safely. And remember to do it, so they don't think you've fallen in a ditch somewhere.
- Don't park your bike in a dodgy, badly lit area. It may be scary to retrieve it after dark and could leave it more vulnerable to thieves.
- Put your lock key and lights at the top of your bag so you can unlock your bike and get away quickly. You can also use detachable lights to see your way when unlocking in the dark.
- If you cycle a lot by night, take spare batteries, spare lights or opt for rechargeable lights.
- Be extra vigilant on the roads, looking out for drunk pedestrians and drunk drivers.
- If you are dressing up, consider the cycle-ability of your outfit before you leave the house. Pencil skirts and platform heels may look great at the bar but could be a battle on the bike. See *Cycle in style* (p138).
- Hi-viz clothing and accessories can be fun in a nightclub and there are some great brands around that offer stylish alternatives to traditional hi-viz anoraks.

- If it's not too far and you feel safe or are with someone, walk and push. The bike might even keep you upright and you can put your front light on to guide the way.
- Depending on how friendly your bartender/ landlord is, you could your bike inside the pub and come back to get it the next day.
- Invest in a folding bike. Just make sure you're not too drunk to fold it.
- Try to avoid leaving your bike out all night but, if there's no other option, find well-lit bike parking with CCTV, and lock the wheels, saddle and frame – or take removable parts with you. Be sure to carry cable locks as well as a D lock so you can lock the bike as securely as possible.

Bike rides for pleasure

The humble bike ride – it's the perfect way to enjoy your own company as well as the company of friends and family. It's also an ideal pace at which to travel, covering more ground than you would by walking and being able to appreciate your surroundings much more than you would by car. Here are a few tips to make the most of the experience:

- Giving a bike ride a final destination or activity can make it much more fun and rewarding, whether it's a trip to a vintage fair, food market, picnic spot or a dip in a lake. Combining a bike ride with something you love will give the trip a satisfying structure that's tailor-made just for you.
- When cycling in groups, check everyone is at a similar level or that there's a general consensus about speed and stop-offs. If you have speed-loving Sue, who wants to

beat her personal best, in a group with whimsical Winnie, who likes taking pictures of everything she sees, it's going to be frustrating for all.

- Set yourself realistic distances. A circular route is best, unless you can make other arrangements for travelling home, like getting a train.
- If you want a relaxed ride with inexperienced cyclists or kids, plan your route and avoid busy roads – not only can it be stressful, but people can get left behind at traffic lights. Coastal or river paths are great as they are scenic and flat.
- Make sure you take snacks and plenty of fluids, even if you're planning on stopping for lunch.

Cycling holidays

Whether it's a two-week cycling tour of the Rockies or a cycle/shopping weekend to Paris, cycling holidays can be a great way to discover new places, set yourself a challenge and catch a few rays of sunshine along the way. A hassle-free method is to book through a cycle-holiday company; they will plan your route, sort out the logistics and even provide the bikes. But, if you fancy organizing it yourself, here are a few tips:

- Plan your route
Route finding has been revolutionized by the GPS function on smartphones, but fumbling with your phone as you cycle can be awkward and dangerous. If you don't want to fork out for a cycling sat nav or Garmin, try a simple little device called the Incredible Bike Band, which attaches your smartphone

to your handlebars, keeping it viewable and stable. Or, if you are navigating, old-school-style, with a paper map, try keeping it in a small shoulder bag on your person or, if you don't mind the nerdy tourist look, you could try a waterproof map case around your neck.

• Always pre-book accommodation
If staying in city hotels, check that they can store bikes. Small hotels on busy streets will not always have space, meaning you have to park on the street, which could be risky if you have an expensive bike.

• Consider transport options
If you're taking your own bike abroad, plan how you are going to get it there and back.

Bikes have to be dismantled and packed away. If you are cycling to a destination but flying back, either take a bike bag with you or find out where you can buy one at your destination. Otherwise, you might find yourself in a world of pain, trying to get your bike through check-in. Likewise, don't assume trains will always let you on with your bicycle – always check in advance.

• Learn the lingo
Make a note of bike vocabulary in the language of the country you are going to. You might find it hard to mime 'inner tube' to a bemused bike-shop worker in Barcelona.

PROFILE
Emily Chappell, London and
around the world
Blog: thatemilychappell.com

On September 1 2011 I left to cycle around
the world. For the three years before that, I
worked as a cycle courier in London, England,
and blogged about it at thatmessengerchick.
wordpress.com. I've never enjoyed a job so
much, or stuck with it so long, but there's
very little career development in couriering,
so I'm delighted to have found something
else that enables me to cycle and write full-
time. (Luckily, I never wanted to be rich.)

What bike do you ride and why do you like it?
My current bike is a custom-built expedition
tourer by Oak Cycles, and I love it because it's
carried me reliably over thousands of miles
of mountains and deserts, and because it is
absolutely unique, designed solely for me and
for this ride, covered in memories (and dust),
and will be with me for the rest of my life.

Why do you love cycling and how does it benefit your life?
That's a difficult question to answer
concisely. Cycling takes up so much of my
life that I can't imagine where or what I'd
be without it. Thanks to the bicycle, I have
discovered my dream job (cycle courier),
come of age as a writer, cycled across a huge
chunk of the planet, met some of the most
important people in my life and fallen in love
with the sense of strength, capability and
independence cycling gives me.

Tell me about the highs and lows of your trip around the world.
I haven't done the whole world yet – it's still
a work in progress! But so far there have
definitely been more highs than lows. One
of the main joys of my trip has been all the
wonderful people I've met, and the kindness
and hospitality I've constantly encountered.
The world is a much friendlier place than I
expected, and I've lost a lot of my cynicism.
The lows were predictable things like
headwinds, rain, saddlesore and exhaustion,
but you always forget the pain once it's over.

Do you have any tips for cycling such long distances?

The obvious one would be to go at your own pace – some people enjoy racing along at 200 kilometres per day, but others find they're happier covering just 50 kilometres, and spending more time drinking tea, admiring the scenery and making friends. Neither approach is better, but they will lead to very different experiences. My journey included some very fast stages, and some very slow ones, and I couldn't really tell you which I preferred. There are a lot more tips on my website but, once you start off, you'll discover that cycle touring is ultimately a very simple – and flexible – business.

How do you carry stuff on your bike and what is essential kit?

I have four panniers, a rack pack and a Bar Bag (which contains essentials like my passport and toothbrush, and would be the first thing I'd rescue from a burning tent). Most of what I'm carrying is 'essential', in that I don't have space for anything I could do without, but my tent and sleeping bag are probably the most vital – being able to camp gives me a lot more flexibility, saves me money and ensures I never have to worry too much about finding somewhere to sleep.

GET INVOLVED – ORGANIZED RIDES AND EVENTS

Naked rides, charity rides, city rides, country rides, rides to admire scenery, rides to admire each other – if you want to join an organized bike ride or get involved with an event, it won't take long to find one that suits you.

Three alternative bike rides

1. The Tweed Run

The first Tweed Run took place in London in 2009. Needless to say, a trend was set and similar rides now take place in cities and towns all over the world. The basic idea is to get dressed up in a tweedy or vintage outfit and embark on a group jaunt with similarly attired cyclists. It's tweed jackets and plus fours aplenty, along with flat caps, pipes and pocket watches. Vintage dresses are also in abundance and bicycles are given vintage makeovers, with the odd penny-farthing

making an appearance. The popularity of these rides is a clear indicator that cyclists like to embrace cycling's rich and wonderful history and salute the cycling fashions of yesteryear. Prizes are awarded for Most Dapper Chap, Most Dashing Dame, and Best Moustache, with stop-offs for tea and cake, and general showing-off, along the way.

2. Critical Mass

Critical Mass has now been going for over 20 years and takes place in over 300 cities around the world. It involves an unlimited number of cyclists meeting at a certain point in the city on a Friday evening and cycling en mass through the streets, taking control and 'being the traffic'. The aims of Critical Mass have changed and evolved over the years, as you would expect from a supposedly 'leaderless' movement that takes place in so many diverse cities, but the overall vibe is about empowerment for urban cyclists. Critical Mass has ignited public controversy and conflict with the authorities in some areas but the mood is generally positive and sociable.

Tips for longer rides

- Make sure you do some training in advance, but don't attempt a long ride the day before – last-minute training will only make you tired and achy on the day.

- Be prepared to cycle among crowds. This can be slow-going at times but the bonus is you're unlikely to get lost and the atmosphere is sociable and uplifting.

- Organize how you will get to and from the ride before you book it. Check it's on a train route and that trains are running that weekend (and accepting bikes) or that there is a designated driver and room for all your bikes and gear.

- Padded cycle shorts are essential, as are muesli bars and lots of fluids.

3. World Naked Bike Ride

The World Naked Bike Ride is a mass ride where, you guessed it, people get naked. But the WNBR movement stands for a lot more than just swinging your bits around on your bike. The point of the ride is fundamentally environmental. Riders often paint their bodies with combinations of pretty patterns and political slogans, protesting against cars, greed and wealth, and championing green lifestyles, love and peace.

The rides are known for their sense of celebration and party atmosphere, and there is no pressure to completely strip off. So, invest in a comfy saddle, get your body-paints out and, as the organizers say, 'Go as bare as you dare!'

Other ways to get involved

Cycling clubs have been going since the birth of cycling, proving bike riders have a natural tendency to want to be sociable and cycle together, and it's reassuring to know they are still very much going strong. There are a wide variety of clubs out there; some may be sport-orientated but they're not exclusive to the seasoned professional. Many welcome cyclists of all abilities and are keen to encourage families and children to get involved. You usually pay a low annual fee to join and are then invited to group rides and various events. They can be great if you want cycling to be a regular weekend activity, and want to build up a bit of fitness and make a few chums along the way. If you are interested in joining a club, you should find a local option pretty quickly with a little bit of internet research. Have a think about what type of cycling you want to do, so you can find a crowd that are on a similar wavelength.

Local campaign groups and coalitions both organize rides and events, and also get involved with the politics and planning of cycling in the area. Depending on their size, they may have full-time staff but will be largely made up of volunteers. They work with governments and other stakeholders to advocate better cycling facilities and cyclists' rights. If you want to get involved with cycle-planning matters at a grassroots level, this is a constructive way to get your voice heard. As a member of the London Cycling Campaign, I have attended brain-storming sessions and large conferences with transport ministers,

as well as casual pub drinks. And I once attended a fashion show, followed by a fancy-dress bike ride along the beach, organized by the Santa Barbara bike coalition, when visiting the US.

Off-beat bicycle activities

- Bicycle polo: Bike polo has actually been around since the 1890s but has made a comeback in recent years as an urban hobby in many countries all over the world.

- Bicycle ballet: Whether it's jaw-dropping balletic acrobatics on a moving bicycle or group dance/bicycle workshops for kids, bikes and dance have a stronger synergy than you might think.

- Cycling music festivals: In San Francisco, the Bicycle Music Festival is run entirely on pedal power; while, in the New Forest in England, the Early Riser Festival combines plenty of tracks and routes to tie in with a stellar line-up of musical acts.

- Pedal-powered cinemas: Watch your favourite film from the comfort of your saddle. Yes, some clever people have created mobile cinemas that are entirely powered by the audience's pedalling.

- Pedal-powered mobile pubs: Same as the cinema, but it's a mobile pub… Yes, a Dutch invention that allows up to 17 people to sit and pedal and drink on a bar-shaped vehicle. One person must remain sober to steer the drunken ship!

CYCLING AND COMMUNITY

The blogger community and cycling sites

When I first got back into cycling and was inspired by the positive impact it had on my life, I wanted to tell people about it. After boring friends and family, I knew I needed a further reach and overcame my internet incompetence to start a blog. I eagerly posted my pictures and ponderings and was pleasantly surprised that there were people who were interested and wanted to talk back. It wasn't long before I was cycling around the city to meet like-minded types for coffee, and attending events and rides. A whole new network had opened up to me.

The bloggersphere's power for international communication is immense and I have connected with many fellow bloggers from all over the world. By browsing through cycling blogs from different cities, you can learn a great deal about their cycling culture and the landscape. So get out there and start your own blog – trust me, it's a lot of fun.

Camaraderie

I have made lots of friends through cycling: close friends whom I now can't imagine living without (my rock-solid business partner and friend Lavinia) and people I have only met once but with whom I've had utterly engaging conversations and liked straight away. In one of the latter encounters, the chap I was talking to said, 'Most people who like bikes are nice people.' Maybe it's just the nice ones who talk to each other or maybe it's the bond of sharing common ground and a similar outlook, I don't know, but in my experience it is true. Bicycle people are nice people.

There's a physical openness to cycling that encourages interaction. I am not anti-driving, but the cover of a car is obstructive and anti-social, hindering communication – often you just about make out the face and recognize a smile, but not much else. Cyclists see each other clearly and, as long as they are not wearing balaclavas, they can read each other's expressions. When cycling one winter, it suddenly started snowing and I was in awe at how pretty and magical it felt. As I passed another cyclist, we shared a look that was somewhere between, 'Are we mad cycling in the snow?' And, 'Oh, isn't it pretty!' I wouldn't have exchanged such nuances in emotion with a fellow driver had I been in a car. And I don't think we would have connected in the same way if we had both been on foot, either. Perhaps what encourages communication among cyclists is the cohesiveness of being in a minority.

Cycling for change

Being in a minority with a strong vision for change is a powerful force, and already the cycling community has achieved great things. Who would have thought, ten years ago, that there would be city-wide cycle-hire schemes like the Paris Vélib in London and New York?

Of course, as we cycle about, day to day, we are not thinking of bicycles as a catalyst for change, we are thinking about our lives and our work – but when you stop and reflect on how far we've come and how much momentum around cycling is still building, it's exciting. And it feels good to be excited about something and part of something that has such positive potential.

In a world where the common outlook is that things are getting progressively worse, not better, cycling, over time, could significantly shift the balance. This is something we can all do to reduce our carbon footprints, to improve our health and well-being and to be more sociable in our communities. The new world of cycling is deeply intertwined with technology and the arts, leading to huge potential for a growth in enterprise and jobs. So do your bit and get on your bike. You might not think it at the time, but you could be helping to make the world a better place.

Jools Walker (aka Lady Velo), London >>>
Blog: velo-city-girl.blogspot.com

I live and cycle in London. The scene here is fantastic; there's such an eclectic mix of cyclists around the city, making it really vibrant and fun. The cycling community is friendly, welcoming and a joy to be a part of. Cycling has made me fitter, healthier and happier! It's also encouraged me to meet and make new friends . . . I can be quite the introvert at times . . . It's brought me out of my shell. I cycle for both leisure and work . . . It's such a massive part of my life, it's hard to imagine not being on my bike for either!

CYCLING WITH LITTLE ONES

Transporting your children by bike can be hugely practical, not to mention heaps of fun for all involved. It can tick many boxes for a busy parent: getting your little cherubs out in the fresh air, seeing their faces light up and hearing their squeals of delight as they discover the joys of travelling by bike and (with the rose-tinted glasses removed) getting them from home to nursery and back without any bawling, dawdling or buggy battles.

And for those mums who, pre-baby, cycled wherever they went, don't despair; it won't be long until you can get back in the saddle.

As soon as your nipper can sit up straight, you can get them on the bike. I first got my daughter, Florence, on board the bike with me when she was 14 months old and it's been invaluable to me as a parent and lots of fun for her. Here is the lowdown on the best bits of kit to securely pedal the wee ones from A to B.

Important note: I have listed age ranges and weights for different seats below (and different brands may also specify their own ranges), but obviously all children vary and parents should always use their own discretion. Only use the ages given as a rough guide, and consider what works for your own child and you. Never exceed the maximum weight given by specific products, however.

Teaching your child to ride a bike

Children usually learn to ride a bike around the age of five. Some may be ready to learn as early as three. The key is for them to master the balance, so, while you might be tempted to strap on the stabilizers as your parents probably did with you, the modern approach is to avoid them altogether. You can start with a 'balance bike' from around 18 months, when a child is stable on their feet. A balance bike has no pedals, so the child learns to glide by pushing themselves along. Or, for older children, try lowering the saddle, so the child can put their feet on the ground, and taking the pedals off, effectively creating your own balance bike; you can then add the pedals back on when you think your child is ready.

'With my first child, I did stabilizers on his bike and a tag along on my bike. He became dependent on the support and it was six months until he could go it alone. With my second, I didn't bother with stabilizers; I let her sit on the bike at home to get used to it and then took her to the park, literally pushed her off, told her to pedal and ran along holding the scruff of her neck . . . She mastered it in three days.' Jane Smith, London, UK

Front-mounted child seats

Age range: 9 months to 3 years (maximum weight: 15kg).

Position: The child sits on a front seat with legs under the handlebars, while Mum reaches her arms around. Children can get too big before they get too heavy in this position. If they can't fit their legs under the handlebars, it's a struggle to see over their head as you ride or you can't get a good grip on the handlebars, they're too big.

How do they attach? These seats are easy to attach, usually with a mounting bracket that is clamped on to the handlebar or handlebar stem. The seat than clicks into the bracket and can be easily removed (the bracket stays on the bike). Utility bikes/city hybrids are a good bicycle for these child seats, as the riding position and height of the handlebars allow more space for the child.

Pros:
- The child is in a secure position and in full view between your arms – good for both parent and child, as you don't have to twist round to talk to them or check on them and they feel more secure.
- Great view for the child – being up front, they can see what's going on – and a great introduction to the joys of cycling.
- Easy to attach to most bikes.

Cons:
- Some parents report they have to cycle bow-legged to avoid contact with the seat. This is not always the case, though, so test ride the seat with your bike before you buy.
- If you push yourself forward on your bike to get going, your tummy may collide with the seat, so you have to adjust to a gentler push-off.

The test ride: I introduced my daughter to the world of cycling with a front-mounted seat and we both loved it. As she was still quite little, having her between my arms felt like a reassuringly secure position and she always seemed very content to be up front. Steering felt fine, but you had to be careful when parking up and dismounting, to make sure that the bike was stable and the handlebars didn't swing round with the weight. It was a sad day when her little legs got too big to fit underneath the handlebars. The only criticism I have of this seat is that it didn't last long enough (Florence fitted in it for 15 months).

Rear-mounted child seats

Age range: 9 months to 6 years (maximum weight: 22kg).

How do they attach? These seats either attach to the rear rack or have a mounting bracket that clamps on to your seat tube. The seat then has poles that slot into the bracket and hold it firmly in place. I would suggest a strong and stable utility bike or city hybrid with a rear rack, especially if the child is 10 kilograms or more. These seats tend to be quite bulky as they have to support the child and ensure they can't fall out. You can get rear seats for children of five years or over that are of a simpler, lighter construction.

Pros:
• Higher maximum weight and more space than a front seat, so your child can use it for longer.
• Easy to get hold of and reasonably priced.
• Adjustable feet holders to cater for your growing child.

Cons:
• Sometimes you can't use with panniers on the back of your bike, as these seats may cover the rack completely.
• It's difficult to chat or check your child is OK, as you have to twist around to do so.
• Cycling with an empty child seat can be annoying as it may bounce and rattle. On the plus side, as long as you tighten the straps securely, you can carry a whole load of shopping in them when your child is elsewhere.

The test ride: Florence and I have used a rear seat since she was two and a half, and we still use it now at four and a half years old. It's very convenient for regular trips as it gets us to our destination much quicker than walking or taking the buggy (two to four being the age when most kids outgrow the buggy but get tired easily when walking). The problem I have with it is when dismounting – you have to shift the bike and get it leaning against something stable to get your child off safely and this is quite a strain with a growing girl and a heavy bike. My daughter has never liked it as much as the front-mounted seat. This may be to do with that fact she is staring at my back – not an ideal position for a very chatty, attention-seeking four-year-old, but I am confident it will last her until she is ready for her own bike.

Trailers

Age range: These are normally categorized by weight rather than age, but I would say they're suitable for kids between roughly one and four years old. You can get

single or double trailers, with some of the better quality models taking around 30 kilograms. As they have a hood, it's a good idea to test-ride for older children to check there's enough head room when it's pulled down.

How do they attach? Trailers come with a hitch that bolts on to the hub of the rear wheel; the arm of the trailer then clicks into the hitch, and a safety strap connects to the frame and the trailer arm. They usually come with a brightly coloured flag that extends up from the trailer to improve visibility.

Pros:
- The double-seated trailers can transport two children and often have space for shopping.
- They are covered, so your child is protected from rain, wind and sun.
- You don't feel the weight as you would with a child on a rear seat on the bike, which also makes it easier to balance and less hard work.

- You can attach it to your own bike rather than forking out for a cargo bike.
- Getting your kids in and out is easier and involves less lifting.
- Children have more space than on a bike seat, so can bring a teddy, blanket or snack and get comfy.

Cons:
- Your children are low down and behind you, so it doesn't feel quite as safe and reassuring as having them up front in full view.
- Detaching and folding down the trailer can be a chore.
- You need to take extra care going downhill as the weight behind you can propel you forward.
- Some of the cheaper models don't have much suspension, so it can be a bumpier ride for your little ones.
- Kids can get up to mischief or squabble, as they are in their own little den and Mum is busy cycling.

The test ride: I used a trailer for a month when visiting the US. My daughter was two and, despite me feeling nervous about her being both behind me and somewhat separated from me, it actually worked very well. She loved it, as it was her little domain, and it was surprisingly smooth and easy to cycle with. I did have the luxury of cycling on very wide, straight and quiet residential roads, and a garage to store it in – a luxury I don't have living in a city flat. However, if I ever had two little ones, I would consider a trailer, especially for colder, rainier times of year.

Cargo bikes

Cargo bikes are commonplace in Holland and Denmark and are gradually growing in popularity in other parts of the world. They are basically a large utility bike with a big cargo box attached at the front (and a smaller front wheel and elongated frame to accommodate it).

How do they attach? They are already attached, that's the beauty of it: there's no faffing; they are built and ready to go. The box has seats and safety straps, so they're safe and sound when cycling on road.

Age range: 6 months to approximately 8 years.

Pros:
• You can carry two kids and lots of other shopping etc.
• Kids are up front in a fun, sociable and secure position.

• Easy for everyday use as there's nothing to attach, you simply get on and go.
• There is a stand that you kick down when you stop, so you don't need to lean it against something.

Cons:
• It's a big unit and could be tricky to store at home or find a place to park when you're out and about.
• It's a cumbersome, heavy number, so cycling is slow and steady; you can't nip through traffic or pick up too much speed.
• They are expensive.

The test ride: I was very excited to finally have another go on a cargo bike, having admired them and all their practical potential for a few years now. My daughter and her friend hopped in and off we went, both of them giggling away as I got to grips with steering. They are definitely a fun way to get around! You get smiles as you go and your kids are in full view, and you have a comfy riding position. They're not cheap, so it's a big commitment but, if you use it every day for the school run and shopping, you'll find that, over a couple of years, the initial outlay will be less than the cost of petrol or public transport tickets, and the financial, health and environmental rewards will make it worth your while.

'Almost always, the creative dedicated minority has made the world better.'
Martin Luther King, Jr.

PROFILE
Julie Roebuck, Holland

What's the cycling scene like in Holland?

In the Netherlands, cycling is maybe seen a little differently – getting on a bike here is as everyday as getting dressed, eating and drinking.

What bike do you ride and why do you like it?

It depends if my son is with me, which bike I use. Mostly I use the Omafiets (Dutch-style bike) when I'm alone but, as there's no child seat, I have to use the Bakfiets/cargo bike when I'm with my son. For holidays and for a morning out cycling somewhere, I do have a hybrid, which is slightly lighter and will pull a child car behind, but that's not used more than a couple of times a year; it's a hobby bike. The practicality is why I like them – I like the Bakfiets more nowadays mostly because I can carry the shopping and child and anything else in the box.

What do you love about cycling and how does it benefit your life?

I couldn't manage without the bikes as I do everything by bike: bring my son to the crèche, go to work, go into town shopping, a night out. Basically all journeys in or around the city, and so much time is saved. It's not something I really think twice about though; it's more of a decision when not to cycle. So I guess it benefits my life in that I can't live without it and would have to get public transport or drive, which are pretty impractical and take longer. Plus, why would you drive, or walk for that matter, to the supermarket when it's at the end of the street? Call me lazy, but shopping bags are heavy!

How to . . .
Cycle to keep fit

Cycling is the perfect way for busy women to keep fit, especially if you struggle to get exercise into your regular routine. This chapter covers the fitness benefits of general cycling and the different disciplines you can engage in, as well as providing tips on stretching exercises and stylish fitness gear. All that's left for you to do is get pedalling!

As a child, I was sporty: netball, gymnastics, athletics, swimming . . . a jack-of-all-sports kind of a girl. But then I left school and life got in the way. And, although I would often still think of myself as 'sporty', eventually I realized that, since I now did no sport apart from the occasional swim, this was no longer true and I reluctantly deleted my sporty credentials from my CV.

Not having an opportunity to exercise frustrated me. Like many young adults, I had started working full time in an office and spent many hours with my bottom attached to a swivelling chair. My weekends were social but not sporty, unless dancing on tables into the small hours of the morning counts.

When I first started cycling to work, I was overjoyed that I had finally found a way to fit exercise into my life and sustain it. I didn't need to find extra hours in the week; I didn't have to sign up to anything, pay up front for

anything or rely on others. All I needed was my bike.

Cycling improves your health and fitness in five ways:
• Burns calories to keep you trim without having to cut out too much cake!
• Keeps your heart healthy.
• Strengthens and tones your body.
• Improves your mental well-being.
• Wards off illness, especially through not having to share germs with people on public transport.

CYCLING: THE BENEFITS

Burn calories

Cycling is a great way to burn calories and doesn't require you to be amazingly fit. Cycling is relatively low impact, so you can

do it for longer, burning off more calories, than more strenuous sports like running. It's also easier on your joints, so there's less chance of strains or injury.

How many calories you burn off will depend on how much you weigh, how fast you are cycling and how many hills you encounter. Check your weight and speed against this chart and you should get an idea of how many calories you are burning in one hour of cycling.

An easy way to gauge the average speed you cycle at is to look up a trip you do regularly on Google Maps and pinpoint the exact distance, then time yourself. With a bit of help from the calculator, you can then work out what your average speed in miles per hour would be: divide 60 by the number of minutes it takes you to travel the distance, and multiply that figure by the number of miles you travelled. For example, if it has taken you 15 minutes to cycle 4 miles, it is:

$$60 \div 15 \times 4 = 16\text{mph}$$

SPEED OF CYCLING (MPH)	WEIGHT (STONE)				
	7 ST	8 ST	9 ST	10 ST	11 ST
Under 10	178 KCAL	203 KCAL	229 KCAL	254 KCAL	279 KCAL
10–11.9	267 KCAL	305 KCAL	343 KCAL	381 KCAL	419 KCAL
12–13.9	356 KCAL	406 KCAL	457 KCAL	508 KCAL	559 KCAL
14–15.9	445 KCAL	508 KCAL	572 KCAL	635 KCAL	699 KCAL
16–19	533 KCAL	610 KCAL	686 KCAL	762 KCAL	838 KCAL

The suggested daily intake for the average woman is 2,000 calories. Here's the calorie count on a few meals and snacks to give you an idea of how many calories your cycling trips cater for.

CAPPUCCINO	75 KCAL
2 × SLICES OF TOAST WITH BUTTER	164 KCAL
40g BAR OF MILK CHOCOLATE	205 KCAL
A BOWL OF PASTA WITH PESTO SAUCE	384 KCAL
SMALL GLASS OF WHITE WINE	130 KCAL
AVERAGE SLICE OF CHOCOLATE CAKE	235 KCAL

If you want to be more accurate, you could invest in a cycling computer, or download a free app, like Strava, to your smartphone. Strava will tell you the distance you covered, calories burned, mark your progress on the map and your average weekly distance – as well as plotting your personal bests on different sections of the road, alongside other people's times. It does tend to be the domain of the MAMIL (middle-aged man in Lycra) or even VOMIT (very old man in tights) – who might take ridiculous risks trying to cycle that bit faster than the other bloke at work. Yawn. But you needn't go bananas; used well, it can be a fantastic motivational tool – and spur you on to get fitter. Who knows – you might end up winning a Queen of the Mountains badge on your way to work!

On your bike!

The World Health Organization states that adults aged 18–64 should do 150 minutes (2.5 hours) of moderate-intensity aerobic physical activity a week, or 75 minutes of vigorous-intensity exercise.

Raise your hand if you are not getting in your weekly quota . . . but don't worry, the humble bicycle is here to help.

Cycling is an ideal form of moderate-intensity aerobic exercise. A very slow amble on a bike might not get you there but light to moderate cycling, where you start to feel warmer and breathe faster, will. If you want to step up to vigorous intensity, the answer is simple: cycle faster and tackle some hills. Cycling has the added bonus of boosting your metabolic rate and it stays high for some hours after you've finished exercising. So you are still burning at a faster rate when you've locked your bike and are putting your feet up at home.

But how is all this cycling helping?

1. Sleep better
It sounds obvious, but activity during the day helps you to sleep more deeply and soundly. Morning exercise has been shown to improve sleep and mood, but it is late afternoon and early evening when exercise seems to be the most beneficial. Thus, cycling to and from work is the perfect antidote for insomniacs among us.

2. Be calmer
Part of the reason that exercise helps you sleep is that it's a great reliever of stress. We all have stressful lives, but exercise will help you cope with that stress and channel it positively. Cycling keeps you calmer, happier and saner!

3. Look younger
Fresh air does wonders for your complexion, not to mention your outlook on life. Exercise will keep you leaner and younger than any bogus beauty treatment.

4. Be smarter
A little exercise pumps blood and oxygen into your brain, keeping your grey matter healthy and releasing endorphins, which keep you alert and on the ball.

5. Bunk off
Regular exercise boosts you immune system, so, if you're never ill, you'll have to take those 'sick' days as your reward. Just saying . . . why be penalized for your amazing health!

6. Be happy
See all of the above.

Interval training on the commute

Interval training involves a combination of high- and low-intensity bursts of exercise, interspersed with rest periods. It's used by athletes in training as an effective way to build up cardiovascular fitness and improve strength and speed over relatively short periods of training. The benefits of sprint interval training far outweigh a much longer, gentle jog, for example.

So, if you want to take your fitness up a notch, why not use your commute as your very own interval-training programme. Instead of getting frustrated with the inevitable stopping and starting of urban cycling, relish the periods when you can really accelerate and go for it, and enjoy the rest moments at red lights, roundabouts and pedestrian crossings. It's a great way to reach vigorous-intensity levels of exercise – and overall you'll get into work far quicker!

Here are a few tips for making it work:

• Use long stretches with good cycle lanes and no junctions to pick up speed.

• Give yourself a specific point to cycle fast until and, traffic permitting, keep pedalling hard until you get there.

• Take a hillier route; use the hill climbs as the high intensity and cruise downhill for the low intensity.

• Vary the use of your gears – give yourself some high-intensity spin using the lower gears, and some resistance training by notching up into the highest gear.

• Use apps like mapmyride.com, Strava or a cycle computer to track your timing. Set yourself targets for improvement on your average speed, top speed and miles per week, and try to reach a new personal best in something each week.

• Do bursts of cycling with your bum off the saddle and then sit back down – again, this varies the tempo and the muscle groups used. You'll look a bit less idiotic if you do this as you set off at the lights, rather than midway down a quiet street . . . but then, who cares what people think?

• Think of your core strength – keep your back completely straight (especially on the hardest sections), your stomach pulled in and your pelvic floor engaged. This posture will work your glutes (bum muscles), strengthen and tone your core and, in doing so, make you cycle more efficiently.

It's vitally import that you don't let your speed put you in any danger on the road. Always make sure you are paying attention to the surrounding traffic. Ensure you feel in control at all times and that you can brake and stop safely if needed.

Strengthening and toning

Cycling is great for toning and strengthening your thigh, calf and bum muscles. But don't panic, this doesn't mean your thighs will be bursting through your Levi's; moderate cycling combined with stretching exercises will burn fat and define muscles rather than build up muscle bulk.

Strong, toned legs not only look good in shorts but are also a great asset in life. Whether you're climbing mountains or coping with the rigors of motherhood, life is full of physical challenges. A strong body and strong legs are a big help.

Tips for toning:

• Check your saddle is the right height: Place the centre of your foot on the pedal on the down stoke and check your leg is almost fully extended (i.e. you can still apply pressure on the pedal). If your saddle is too low, you will not be working the muscles fully and you could cause a knee injury by putting too much pressure on the knee when it's bent.

• Check your feet are in the right position on the pedal: It should be the balls of your feet that push down on the pedals when cycling.

Which muscles do the work?

The size of each different coloured area shows the relative amount of power each muscle produces.

Your quads do most of the work as you push down towards the floor, then your glutes and calves take over as you reach the bottom of the wheel. Your hamstring sweeps the pedal behind you and your hip flexors help lift the pedal back to the top.

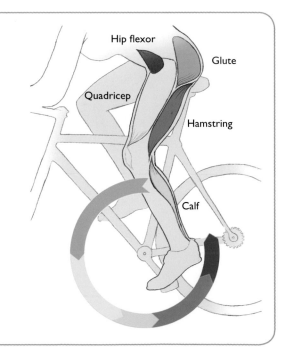

Hip flexor

Glute

Quadricep

Hamstring

Calf

- **Keep pedalling:** Although you may need to coast from time to time, try to keep pedalling as much as possible to give your legs the best workout.

- **Stretch:** Do stretching exercises before you ride to warm up muscles, and then again after you ride to stretch muscles out (see below).

- **Join a yoga class:** It's a great way to strengthen the core as well as stretch out leg muscles that have been working hard.

Stretch yourself

Here are three great stretches to do before and after your ride.

2. Hamstring stretch
Lean forward into your outstretched leg and lift up your toes. You should feel the stretch through the back of your thigh.

1. Quad/hip flexor stretch
Pull your foot up towards you bottom while jutting your hips forward.

3. Calf stretch
Lean into the wall and push down into the heel of your back leg.

'Lack of activity destroys the good condition of every human being, while movement and methodical physical exercise save it and preserve it.'
Plato

Yoga and cycling

Yoga is a great way both to stretch and strengthen the muscles involved in cycling. Here are some perfect postures from professional yoga teacher, Dipa Trivedi, founder of Yoga Muni, London (yogamuni.com).

1. Downward-facing dog pose

Position yourself on the floor on hands and knees. Set the knees directly below the hips and the hands slightly forward of the shoulders.

Exhale and lift the knees away from the floor, pushing yourself on to the balls of your feet.

Keep the knees slightly bent in the beginning and the heels lifted away from the floor. Lengthen the tailbone away from the back of the pelvis and press it lightly towards the pubis. Against this resistance, lift the sitting bones towards the ceiling. Then, with an exhalation, push the top of the thighs back and stretch the heels on to or down towards the floor, keeping the back and arms straight.

This pose is especially good for cyclists because it strengthens the shoulders and back, undoing the stress created by rounding and straining the upper middle back. It's also a great stretch for the calves.

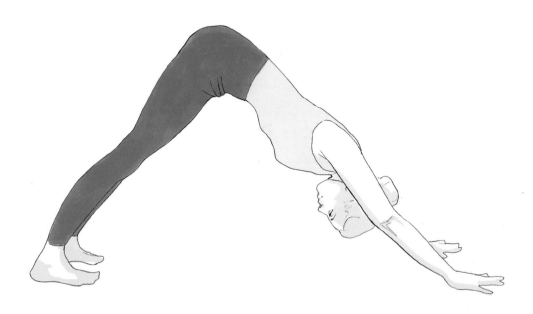

2. Half lord of the fish pose

Sit on the floor with both legs extended forward. Bend the left leg and bring the left foot over to the outside of the right leg, as close to the right hip as possible. Then bring the right arm up and around the left knee. Inhale, lift the torso and rotate to the left, looking over the left shoulder. Repeat on the other side and stay in the posture for 30 seconds to a minute.

This posture helps to stretch out the hip flexors and the glutes, both of which get a workout when cycling.

shoulder blades and the back of your skull into the floor to help give your spine some length. Breathe, relax and stay in the pose for five minutes.

This is a restorative pose, and it helps draw any swelling or tension away from the feet and ankles. It helps prevent varicose veins and relieves any feeling of heaviness in the legs. After a long time working the legs on a bike, it is good to get the blood circulation going again by bringing the legs up the wall. This position will restore tired muscles.

3. Inversion and relaxation: legs up the wall pose

Place a rolled-up blanket or bolster on the floor, against a wall. Sit up so that your right hip is against the wall and, in one motion, swing both legs up the wall, letting your hips sit as close to the wall as is possible. An easy way is to use one's hands on the floor, close to the ears, to push oneself higher up. Let your arms fall out to the sides and press your

TAKE YOUR CYCLING TO THE NEXT LEVEL

Preparing for longer distances

A great way to improve overall fitness through cycling is to set yourself a challenge and sign up for a long-distance ride. Here are some considerations.

Training: Train regularly in the run-up. Start by cycling once a week and then build up to twice or three times. And gradually increase your distances until you are close to the target of the bike ride. If you need some structure and discipline, have a hunt on the internet for a training programme that suits you or train with a friend or group.

Hydration: Drinking plenty of water before, during and after a long ride is essential. When exercising, you lose fluids through sweating and breathing, and you must replenish them to stay strong and healthy. Buy a water-bottle bracket to screw on to your bike and practise reaching for it and drinking while cycling before your big ride. When riding, don't wait until you're thirsty – by this time you are already dehydrated; instead, keep sipping every 20 minutes. Set an alarm on your watch if you are prone to forgetting. Avoid caffeine or alcohol. While both may make you feel good temporarily, they do not hydrate you.

Food: A balanced and healthy diet is recommended to give you the energy and strength you need to keep pedalling for longer periods of time. Cover all the food groups to ensure you have a good balance of carbohydrates, protein, vitamins and minerals. Pay attention to the GI value (Glycemic Index) of foods before, during and after a long ride to ensure you are doing the best to keep your energy levels up. The GI value is the rate at which food causes sugar levels to rise in the blood. Foods with a high GI release glucose more quickly into the blood, so, while they may not be suitable for keeping you going for longer periods, if you need to replace lost energy after hard cycling, high-GI foods can help you. Foods with a lower GI release glucose more slowly, providing a more steady supply, so these foods help to keep you energized for longer.

Morning of ride: Eat food with a low GI to keep your energy level constant, with a mix of carbs and protein. Try fruit/fruit juice, muesli or oat-/bran-based cereal or granary toast with wholenut peanut butter for protein.

During a ride: This is when you need food that can be quickly converted to energy. Energy bars and energy drinks are good. But don't forget to eat 'real' food too, especially if cycling for a long time. Go for something light with carbs and protein, such as sandwiches or rolls followed by an apple or banana.

After a ride: To avoid going weak at the knees after your ride, have a snack to hand. Yoghurt, cheese or milk can be good solutions or jam/honey sandwiches and lots of water.

Cycling indoors

If your training has been scuppered by dark evenings and icy cold conditions, why not bring your bike indoors? Here are three ways to train on your bike without going outside:

Spinning: You can either join a spinning class or just make use of a spinning machine at the gym. This is an exercise machine in the form of a stationary bike and will give you all the benefits of cycling. You will also be able to gauge distance travelled and calories used. A group class can be a great way to ensure you have a fun but disciplined workout.

Turbo-trainers: Use a turbo-trainer to convert your own bike to a stationary exercise bike. It consists of a U-shaped stand that clamps on to the frame and attaches to the rear axle, supporting the back wheel of your bike on a roller. When you pedal, the back wheel spins but the front wheel does not move. You are fully supported, so you can just pedal away while watching TV in the comfort of your own home.

Rollers: Again used with your own bike, rollers take a little more skill to master as the bicycle frame is not connected or supported. They consist of three cylinders (rollers), and the bike quite simply rolls along on top of them. Rollers require balance, and beginners are advised to wear helmets in case they fall. The experience is more true to actual cycling than turbo-trainers or spinning, and racers use rollers to finely tune their balance.

Bicycle disciplines

Want to get competitive from the saddle or observe from the sofa? Here's your guide to the different cycling sports you can take to a professional level.

Road racing: Racing for long distances on a road is probably the most widely recognized cycling sport. It may sound simple, but road racing requires a complex mix of strength, stamina and tactical prowess. Road racing has a history stretching back to the late 1800s and was one of the original Olympic sports in Athens in 1896. The most famous road race is the Tour de France, which was first held in 1903 and averages around 2,230 miles (the route changes year to year). The Italian and Spanish versions, the Giro d'Italia and the Vuelta a España respectively, are also similar lengths.

BMX racing: This consists of eight riders racing around a track 300/400 metres long. The skill is in navigating the small-wheeled bikes over various bumps, jumps and steep corners. BMX racing became an Olympic sport in 2008. Edge-of-the-seat stuff!

Cyclo-cross: A great sport for all abilities; rides are usually no more than an hour and often involve laps of a varied course with hills and other obstacles to overcome. Riders have to dismount at certain points and then jump back on swiftly in the race to get round. Expect mud, excitement and great camaraderie.

Track racing: Track cycling takes place in banked circuits (velodromes), both indoors and outdoors, and involves cyclists racing one another for varying distances. Track racing dates back as far as 1870 but has stood the test of time, still being extremely popular, with a huge fan base at championship level. But it's not just for the professionals; many velodromes hold beginner classes for track newbies to experience the thrill.

Mountain biking: Mountain biking (MTB) requires a strong body and strong nerves. There are two main events at a competitive level: downhill and 4-cross. Downhill is hairy; riders have to get themselves down a rugged hill as quickly as possible and the fastest time wins. In 4-cross, four riders race against each other over bumps and jumps — expect contact, crashes and big personalities.

STYLISH SPORTS GEAR

While the Lycra look has never been my favourite, I do recognize that a vintage dress might not be the best attire for a mud-splattered cyclo-cross race, and sometimes more technical gear is a must.

Techinical gear is a must once you get into competition cycling. Here are some items you may want to look into:

• Padded cycling shorts
These will significantly improve your comfort on long rides. The padded inserts are often referred to as the chamois and will moisture-wick as well as protect. Be sure you get women-specific shorts as the chamois

is placed anatomically so a men's pair may be more of a hindrance than a help. You also want to ensure that the shorts cling tightly to your body – if they are too loose, they may cause chaffing. If you find that regular cycling shorts cut in at the waist or start slipping down, you could opt for bib shorts. These have shoulder straps – a sort of onesie of the cycling world. Again, go women-specific on these, as the design will differ ensuring the straps don't squash your boobs. Take a look at the dhb Aeron ladies' bib shorts – they have the added bonus that the straps unhook, so you can have a quick pee without having to strip off completely.

• A lightweight weatherproof jacket
This will protect you from the elements but won't weigh you down or make you sweat.

Make sure it's breathable as well as waterproof so you don't steam up from within.

• Merino-wool base layers
Insulating, breathable and surprisingly flattering. See *Cycle in style* (p138).

• Cycling shoes
These have cleats that attach to your pedals to make your riding more efficient. Brand suggestions: Specialized and Shimano.

Fortunately, in recent years there have been huge leaps in the style stakes for sporty cycling gear for women, leaving the attitude of 'make it pink and stick a couple of flowers on it' behind.

PROFILE

Anna Glowinski, London, founder
of cycling-wear brand AnaNichoola
Website: ananichoola.co.uk

What kit would you recommend for longer rides and races?

Longer rides and races require different types of kit. In a race, you can assume you are going to get pretty hot pretty quick, so you want tight-fitting clothing for aerodynamics, and fabrics that will absorb moisture away from your body as quickly as possible.

For longer rides, you need to be prepared for the elements and expect your body temperature to fluctuate. Going up hills, café stops, going down hills, being in sheltered or exposed terrain – these all affect your temperature. The key to long rides is layering. Make sure your clothing fits and is comfortable *in your riding position*. When trying garments on, bend over and bend your arms to check everything feels comfortable.

What fabrics do you use and why?

Each layer of clothing has a different function, so each layer needs to be made from a different fabric. However, one thing that is fundamental throughout is breathability of clothing: whether you are trying to cool off or keep warm, you want all the moisture on your skin to be able to escape.

What type of cycling do you do and what bikes do you own?

I am a bike racer of all disciplines; my childhood was spent racing velodrome, road and cyclo-cross. More recently, I have swapped the tarmac for dirt and will commonly be found on a BMX or racing a mountain bike down a mountain.

What do you wear for cycling just out and about?

I am a jeans type of girl, so my outfits will be based around them. If I am going on a journey above, say, ten miles, I will put some Sun Cat Padded Shorts on underneath, and then I will throw on a moisture-wicking T-shirt, like our Stripe Jersey, and for visibility team it with our Hello Yellow Jacket. All these items are perfect for short-distance riding, and you still arrive looking stylish. Oh, and gloves: I never ride without gloves because I *do not* want callouses!

What do you love most about cycling?

My world is cycling and I would be lost without it. It's what all my friends do and what we talk about – it's such a welcoming and friendly sport and that's the best thing.

Little black book of bicycle style

Well, that brings us to the end of *The Girls' Bicycle Handbook*. Below are a few websites and companies to further inspire and inform you ... I truly hope this book has helped you along your bicycling journey and, most importantly, I hope cycling becomes as useful and enjoyable to you as it is to me.

Adeline Adeline: Bike boutique in New York. Adelineadeline.com

Ana Nichoola: Stylish performance cycling gear for women from bike racer and designer Anna Glowinski. Ananichoola.co.uk

Basil: Bicycle bags and baskets. Basil.nl

Bern Unlimited: Stylish, urban bike helmets. Bernunlimited.com

Bike Dock Solutions: Online shop selling a smorgasboard of bike parking and storage solutions. Bikedocksolutions.com

Bobbin Bicycles: Beautiful bicycles and accessories with a vintage twist. Bobbinbikes.co.uk/wordpress

Bowery Lane Bicycles: Very cool bikes and bicycle crates. Bowerylanebicycles.com

Brooks: Classic saddles and accessories. Brooksengland.com

Café du Cycliste: Attractive road cycling gear. Cafeducycliste.com

Cyclechic: Stylish bicycle accessories shipped worldwide. Cyclechic.co.uk

Cyclehoop: Bike parking design at its very best. Cyclehoop.com

Cyclodelic: British-made cycle accessories with a flair for reflective. Cyclodelic.com

Dashing Tweeds: Dashing reflective suits and accessories. Dashingtweeds.co.uk

Dring Dring: Beautiful hand-painted bicycle bells from Canada. Dringdring.ca

Electra: Cool cruisers and a host of accessories. Electrabike.com

Front Yard Company: Modern bike parking. Frontyardcompany.co.uk

Georgia in Dublin: Stylish rainwear by mother-and-daughter team from Ireland. Georgiaindublin.com

H-B Design: Bike parking and storage for your home and community. Hbdesigns.co.uk

Iva Jean: Fashionable, functional bike clothes. Ivajean.com

Knog: Fun and functional bike lights. Knog.com.au

Linus: Stylish bikes and accessories from California. Linusbike.com

Michaux: Beautiful handmade bicycle bags and accessories. Michauxclub.com

Nutcase: Wild and wacky head protection. Nutcasehelmets.com

Pashley: The ultimate in classic bicycles. Pashley.co.uk

Po Campo: Feminine luggage for on and

off the bike. Pocampo.com

Rapha: Coveted cycle apparel brand which now does ladies' gear too. www.rapha.cc

Sawako Furuno: Fantastically feminine helmets. Sawakofuruno.com

Specialized: The experts on women-specific, high-performance bikes and gear. Specialized.com

Tokyobike: City bike brand with beautiful shops in London, Singapore, Berlin, Sydney and Melbourne. Tokyobike.com

Urban Legend: Designer cyclewear made in Budapest. Urbanlegend.cc

Vulpine: Gorgeous merino-wool tops from UK brand. Vulpine.cc

Yakkay: Helmets that look like hats from Denmark. Yakkay.com

Bicycle blogs of note

Toronto
www.416cyclestyle.com
Barcelona
Barcelonacyclechic.blogspot.com
California
Bikeladiesunite.tumblr.com
San Francisco
Bikepretty.com
San Francisco
Bikesandthecity.blogspot.com
San Francisco
Citygirlrides.com
Copenhagen
Copenhagencyclechic.com
Curitiba
Curitibacyclechic.blogspot.com
Taiwan
Fixedgeargirltaiwan.blogspot.com
London

Ispeakbike.blogspot.com
Nashville/Chicago
Letsgorideabike.com
London
Londoncyclechic.blogspot.com
Somerville, MA
Lovelybike.blogspot.com
Santa Cruz
Ridingpretty.blogspot.com
London
Thatemilychappell.com
Portland
Urbanvelo.org
London
velo-city-girl.blogspot.com
New York
Velojoy.com

Rides for the diary

Anjou Velo Vintage: An 87 kilometre bicycle ride through France and a weekend of vintage events. Anjou-velo vintage.com

Critical Mass: Group rides supporting our right to ride on the roads; Critical Mass takes place in hundreds of cities worldwide. Criticalmass.wikia.com

Cycletta: Women-only bike rides in stunning settings all over the UK, supported by Victoria Pendleton. Humanrace.co.uk/events/cycletta

Cyclofemme: A web-based initiative encouraging ladies from all over the world to organize and register a group ride and all step out on their bikes on the same day of the year. Cyclofemme.com

Tweed Rides: Group cycle rides through city streets in vintage wear with frivolities along the way. Search 'tweed ride' + 'your city'

Index

Abroad, taking your bike 189
accessories 48–73
Ana Nichoola 218
Anthony, Susan B. 6

Bags 58–60, 173
cycling-specific 58–9
handbags 60
handlebar 59
messenger 59
rucksacks 59, 176
saddlebags 59
ballet, bicycle 194
Barcelona 182
basket cover 60, 64
baskets 61–5
attaching of to bike 62–3
dog 63–5
KLICKfix 63
metal 62
plastic (wicker effect) 62
things to watch out for 64
wicker 61, 62
bells 61
bespoke bikes 39
bicycle
diagram of parts of a 76–7
impact on liberation
of women 6–7
parts of a 78–83
bicycle disciplines 216
bicycle grief, stages of 114–15
Bike Apple 108
Bike Band 188–9
bike buddy 172
bike bunkers 111
bike fitting 42
bike parking 107, 108–9
bike rack 108
bike stand 111, 112
bike tagging 114
blogs, cycling 17, 140, 195
Bloomer, Amelia 7
bloomers 7
BMX racing 216
Bobbin Bicycles 45
Bobbin Straw Pannier 67
Bonney, Rachel 68
brake pads 78, 84, 87
brakes 78
checking 85, 87
squeaking/grinding 84
breakfast 174
British Rational Dress Society 7
brogues 152
Brooks saddle 83
Brosnan, Jude 54
Budapest 165
Burgueño, Meli 141
Burton, Beryl 10
bus/cycle lanes 132
buying a bicycle 22–47

bespoke bikes 39
cruisers 37
electric bikes 34–5
fixed-gear bike 38
folding bikes 32–3, 110
hybrid bikes 27–9
mountain bikes 31, 136
online 45
questions to ask yourself before
22–3
road bikes 29–30, 42
second-hand bikes 41
size 42
taking a test ride 43
tandem riders 36
utility bikes 26–7

Calories, burning of 204–7
camaraderie 195
canals 130
capes 155, 157
Car Bike Port 108
Cardiff 116
cargo bikes 202
Carrera 56
Carton, Sarah 162
chain/chain area 80
checking 85, 87
cleaning and lubricating 87,
99, 100
putting back on 92
squeaking/clicking/slipping 85
chainset 80, 81
Chappell, Emily 190–1
child seats 199–202
front-mounted 199
rear-mounted 200
children
taking with you on your bike
198–204
teaching them to ride a bike 198
cinemas, pedal-powered 194
city hybrids/bikes 28–9
clothes 18, 20, 146–56, 187
coats/jackets 154–6, 217
for cold weather 162
for cycling to work 173
dresses/skirts 150
shoes 152, 157, 217
tops 148
trousers 146–7
vintage 142–5
wearing in the rain 157, 158
coats/jackets 154–6, 217
cold weather, clothes to wear
in 162
community 195–6
confidence 135, 170
Copenhagen Cycle Chic 140
Coy, Vicky 179
crank arm, checking 87
Critical Mass 192
cruisers 37
culottes 144
cycle chic blogs 17, 140
cycle lanes 132
cycle style see style, cycle

Cycle to Work scheme 170
Cyclechic.co.uk 140
Cyclehoop 109
cycling
barriers 17–19
benefits 12–17, 20
cycling clubs 194
cycling holidays 188–9
cycling safety see road safety
cycling shorts 216–17
Cyclists' Touring Club (CTC) 8
cyclo-cross 216

Daar, Adina 179
d'Antigny, Blanche 8
dark, cycling in the 134, 160–1
Dashing Tweeds 161
Davies, Melissa 39, 141, 152
Denmark 132
derailleur gears 80–1, 92
diet, and long-distance
cycling 214
distance to cycle 172–3
dog baskets 63–5
dogs, tips for cycling with 64
Dorothy cover 60
dresses 143, 150
drinking 134, 186–7
drivetrain 80
cleaning and lubricating 99

Electric bikes 34–5
pedelec 34
twist and go 34
emergency stop 122
Emmison, Sian 45
environment 15

Face wipes 177
fashion 146–56 see also clothes
fitness 12, 14, 204–16
cycling indoors 215
long-distance rides 214
strengthening and toning muscles
210–13
yoga 212–13
Fixa bike shelf 110
fixed-gear bike 38
folding bikes 32–3, 110
frame 42, 79
fresh, staying 176–7
fun, cycling for 184–203
Furuno, Sawako 56

Gears 80–1
changing 122
checking 87
derailleur 80–1, 92
hub/internal 81
Georgia in Dublin 158
Geréby, Zsófi 165
GI (Glycemic Index) 214
Gill, Txell Hernández 182
gloves 72
Glowinski, Anna 218
going out at night 186–8
Grand, Sarah 8–9

Hair, combatting of helmet 180–1
handbag hugger 60
handbags 60
handlebars 42, 79
adjusting height of 93
checking 85, 87
sizes 42
Harberton, Lady 8
hats 163
Haute Réflecture 161
head scarf 181
headset 79, 93
health benefits 204–13
heavy goods vehicles (HGVs)
132–3
helmets 52–7
fitting of 57
and hair 180–1
and safety issue 54–5
types of 55–6
high five exercise 123
Highway Code 121
holidays, cycling 188–9
Holland 26, 132, 203
home, bike security at 112–14
hoods 157
'how to' guides 90–9
hybrid bikes 27–9
city 28–9
sports 29
hydration 214

Indoors
cycling 215
storing your bike 110
insurance 114
interval training 208

Jackets 154–6, 217
Japan 33

Keller, Helen 52, 101
kerb, cycling near the 125–6
King, Dani 11
KLICKfix 63
Knog 70

Lane changing 128
laptops, transporting 173–4
left-hand turns 123, 127
leggings 146, 150
lights 69–70, 134, 174
attaching 69
flashing 69
Knog 70
things to watch out for 69–70
listening 132
Livingstone, Jenny 20
local campaign groups 194
locks/locking 50–1, 104–7
cable 51
chain 51, 104
D 50, 104, 107, 186
folding 51
saddle 51, 83
how to lock your bicycle 107
where to lock it up 107, 109

London Cycling Campaign 194
London Tweed Run 184
Londonderry, Annie 9
long-distance rides 214
looking back 123
lorries 101
lube 85

M check 86–7
maintenance 19, 74–101
    cleaning and lubricating 99
    common noises and what they
        mean 84–5
    handlebar height adjustment 93
    M check 86–7
    mending punctures 95–8, 100
    parts of a bike 78–83
    pumping up tyres 71, 90
    putting your chain back on 92
    removing and installing wheels
        93–4
    saddle adjustment 42, 92
    weekly check (ABCD) 85
make-up 177
merino wool clothing 148, 217
messenger bag 59
Michaux Club 68
Mills, Amanda 39
miniskirt 144
mixte frame 41
mobile pubs, pedal-powered 194
mountain bikes 31, 136
mountain biking (MTB) 216
muscles 210
music festivals, cycling 194

New York 136
night, safety at 134, 160–1, 187
noises 84–5
    after every wheel rotation 84
    chain area squeaking/clicking/
        skipping 85
    clunking/clicking of pedals 84
    rattling/jangling 85
    squeaking/grinding brakes 84
non-drivers, cycling for 121

Off-road practice 118
organized rides 192–4
outdoors, storing bike 110–13
overtaking traffic 128

Pacing 21
panniers 66–7, 173, 184, 186
parking at work 176
parking, bike 107, 108–9
pedal pushers 142
pedals
    checking 87
    clunking/clicking of 84
    positioning of when stopping and
        starting 122
pedestrians 131, 134
Pendleton, Victoria 10–11
Pfeiffer, Michelle 74
Plantlock 112
pleasure, bike rides for 188

polo, bike 194
positioning 125–30
    changing lanes 128
    one metre in from kerb 125–6
    overtaking traffic 128
    primary/central 126
    roundabouts 129–30
    turning left 127
    turning right 127
primary control position 126
Princess Kate bike stand 112
PSI 71, 90
public transport 14
pumps 71, 90
punctures, mending 95–8, 100, 174

Rain, cycling in the 133, 157, 158
Raleigh bicycles 41
Randall, Diane Jones 136–7
reflective accessories 160–1
reflectors 71, 134, 160
right-hand turns 123, 127
road bikes 29–30, 42
road racing 216
road safety 118–37
    in adverse weather conditions
        133–4
    bus/cycle lanes 132
    confidence and state of mind
        134
    cycle lanes 132
    emergency stop 122
    finding quieter roads and
        off-road routes 130
    and HGVs 132–3
    listening 132
    at night 134
    off-road practice 118
    and pedestrians 131
    positioning see positioning
    push rather than panic 130
    safe swerving 123
    signalling and turning 123
    stopping and starting 122
    and traffic 17
Roebuck, Julie 203
roller-racing 215
rollers 215
Roswell, Joanna 11
roundabouts 128, 129–30
rucksacks 59, 176

Saddlebags 59
saddles 42, 45, 82–3, 210
    adjustment of 42, 92
    checking 87
    getting the perfect height 42
    with holes 82–3
    leather 83
    locks 51, 83
    no-nos 83
    wider 82
safety see road safety
San Francisco style 140–1
scarves 163
Scott, Georgia 158
second bike 109

second-hand bikes 41
security 104–17
    bike tagging 114
    at home 112–14
    indoors 110
    outdoors 112–13
    insurance 114
    locks and locking see locks/
        locking
    taking action if bike is stolen 113
sheds 111
shoes 152, 157, 217
shopping 184–6
signalling 123
skirts 150
Smile bike wall anchor 112
Smith, Jane 198
snow, cycling in 134
Sold Secure 50
Somerville, Megan 100–1
spinning 215
sports gear 216–17
sports hybrids 29
sprocket 80
Stanton, Elizabeth Cady 7
state of mind 135
steering 79
stolen bike 113
Stope, Charlotte Carmichael 7
stopping and starting 122
storage of bike 19
    indoors 110
    outdoors 110–12
Strada, Alfonsina 9–10
Strava 206
stretching exercises 211
Strong, Ann 66
style, cycle 138–67
    accessories 163
    colours and coordination 163
    fashion see clothes
    San Francisco 140–1
    sports gear 216–17
    vintage clothes 142–5
    sunglasses 163
    swerving safely 123

Tandem riders 36
Tasmania 20
test rides 43
Tieche, Kirstin 140
Tombs, Emilee 116
toning 210–11
tops 148
Torres, Christina 141
touring bikes 30
track racing 216
traffic, cycling in 17
    see also road safety
trailers 200–1
training 17, 121
Trophy bike holder 110
Trott, Laura 11
trousers 146–7
turbo-trainers 215
turning left 123, 127
turning right 123, 127

Tweed Run 184, 192
tweed suit 143
tyres 78
    checking 85, 87
    checking PSI range 90
    mending punctures 95–0, 100,
        174
    pumping up 71, 90

Urban cycling 101
Urban Legend 165
utility bikes 26–7, 42

Valves 90
vintage clothes 142–5
    1920s dropped waist 143
    1940s tweed suit 143
    1950s dress 144
    culottes 144
    miniskirt 144
    pedal pushers 142

Walker, Jools 196
wall hangings, for bikes 110
water bottles 71–2
waterproofs 72, 157, 158, 174
weather conditions, adverse 133–4
    see also rain, cycling in the
well-being 14
wheels 78
    checking 86–7
    cleaning 99
    mending punctures 95–8, 100,
        174
    regular noise after every rotation
        of 84
    removing and installing 93–4
    see also tyres
wicker baskets 61, 62
Willard, Frances E. 19, 112
wind 134
work, cycling to 168–82
    benefits 168, 170
    combatting helmet hair 180–1
    Cycle to Work scheme 170
    journey length 172–3
    luggage 173
    parking at work 176
    planning of route 170
    practice run 170–1
    preparations 170–1
    route 171–3
    staying fresh 176–7
    transporting laptops 173–4
    wardrobe 173
World Naked Bike Ride (WNBR) 193

Yakkay 56
Yamanouchi, Miki 33, 113
yoga 212–13

ACKNOWLEDGEMENTS

A big thank you to Rachel Bevis, Sian Emmerson and the team at Bikeworks for all your technical bicycle advice. Thank you to Judy Buttris and Bridget Benelam at the British Nutrition Foundation. Thank you to; Evans, Cycle surgery, Tokyo bikes, There Cycling and Just E-bikes for the test-rides. A huge thank you to Kerry Enzor and all the team at Quercus who have been quite simply brilliant! And finally to all the women who talked to me about why they love cycling!

Picture credits

The following abbreviations are used throughout the picture credits:
l = left, r = right, t = top, m = middle, b = bottom.

All images are courtesy of Caz Nicklin unless stated otherwise.

2 © Tom Miles; 4 © Bradford Bird; 6 © Swim Ink 2, LLC/Corbis; 8l The Art Archive/SuperStock; 8r Getty Images; 9l Courtesy of Peter Zheutlin; 10 © TopFoto; 11l WireImage/Getty Images; 11r © Christophe Karaba/epa/Corbis; 13 © Tom Miles; 14 © Tom Miles; 16 © Tom Miles; 23 © Tom Miles; 24 © Bradford Bird; 25 Courtesy of Ivan Jones; 30 © MonsieurVelo, courtesy of Txell Hernández Gil; 33 © Pete Gawlik/Alamy; 35 © Kenya Chiba/Aflo/Corbis; 37 © Transtock/Corbis; 38 © Paula Belil Pires, courtesy of Txell Hernández Gil; 43 © Tom Miles; 44 Courtesy of Bobbin Bicycles; 45 Courtesy of Bobbin Bicycles; 46–7 © Tom Miles; 49 © Tom Miles; 59b Courtesy of New loox; 60 © Tom Miles; 61 Courtesy of Electra; 64 Courtesy of Ivan Jones; 65 © Gemma Booth; 67b Courtesy of Bobbin Bicycles; 68 © Tyson Sadlo; 70t Courtesy of Bobbin Bicycles; 73tl © Grant Robinson/Ana Nichoola; 73tr Courtesy of Day Glow Doris; 73bl © Elena Hermosa/Georgia in Dublin; 75 © Tom Miles; 82t Isabel Pavia/Getty Images; 82b age fotostock/SuperStock; 83 © Jeffrey Blackler/Alamy; 88–9 © Bradford Bird; 91 © Tom Miles; 92 © Tom Miles; 94 © Tom Miles; 98 © Bradford Bird; 102–3 © All Canada Photos/Alamy; 105 © Tom Miles; 106 © Tom Miles; 108l Courtesy of Cyclehoop; 108r DarkShadow/Getty Images; 110 Courtesy of Chrome Ltd; 111 Courtesy of Outline Works Ltd; 112t John Englefield/Front Yard Company Ltd; 112m Courtesy of Bike Dock Solutions; 112b Courtesy of H-B Designs; 115 © Frantisek Staud/Alamy; 117 © Simon Stuart-Miller/Alamy; 119 © Tom Miles; 120 © Tom Miles; 121 © Bradford Bird; 124 © Tom Miles; 131 © Tom Miles; 134 © frans lemmens/Alamy; 135 © Tom Miles; 139 © Tom Miles; 141 Courtesy of James Perrin; 142 © Tom Miles; 143r WireImage/Getty Images; 144l Jay P. Morgan/Getty Images; 144r © Tom Miles; 145 © Tom Miles; 146 © Bradford Bird; 151 © Tom Miles; 153 Courtesy of James Perrin; 155t Courtesy of Bobbin Bicycles; 156tl © Andrea Gáldi Vinkó/Urban Legend; 156tr © Ben Broomfield/Cyclodelic; 156bl © Grant Robinson/Ana Nichoola; 156br © Elena Hermosa/Georgia in Dublin; 159 © Orlagh Ní Arrachtain/Georgia in Dublin; 160t © Ky Katrensky, courtesy of One Two Three Speed; 161b © Reka Nyari, courtesy of Vespertine; 164 © Tom Miles; 169 © Tom Miles; 171 Carlos Alkmin/Getty Images; 172 © Bradford Bird; 175 © Tom Miles; 177 © Tom Miles; 182 © Anthony Lau; 183 © Tom Miles; 185 © Tom Miles; 186 © Tom Miles; 189 raspu/Getty Images; 192l © Mike Goldwater/Alamy; 192r AFP/Getty Images; 193 © Gallo Images/Alamy; 200 © Johan Willner/Etsa/Corbis; 201 © Paula Belil Pires, courtesy of Txell Hernández Gil; 205 Jordan Siemens/Getty Images; 209 © Bradford Bird; 217 © Bradford Bird; 218 © Grant Robinson/Ana Nichoola; 219 © Tom Miles.